GUIDED BY THE LIGHT

FOLLOWING YOUR ANGELIC GUIDES

Compiled by: Jewels Rafter

LWL PUBLISHING HOUSE
Brampton, Canada

Guided By The Light - Following Your Angelic Guides

Copyright © 2016 by LWL PUBLISHING HOUSE
A division of Anita Sechesky – Living Without Limitations Inc.

All rights reserved. No part of this publication may be reproduced, distributed, or transmitted in any form or by any means, including photocopying, recording, or other electronic or mechanical methods, without prior written permission of the publisher, except in the case of brief quotations embodied in critical reviews and certain other noncommercial uses permitted by copyright law. For permission requests, write to the publisher, addressed "Attention: Permissions Coordinator," at the address below.

Anita Sechesky – Living Without Limitations Inc.
asechesky@hotmail.ca
lwlclienthelp@gmail.com
www.lwlpublishinghouse.com

Publisher's Note: This book is a collection of personal experiences written at the discretion of each co-author. LWL PUBLISHING HOUSE uses American English spelling as its standard. Each co-author's word usage and sentence structure have remained unaltered as much as possible to retain the authenticity of each chapter.

Book Layout © 2016 LWL PUBLISHING HOUSE

Guided By The Light - Following Your Angelic Guides
Anita Sechesky – Living Without Limitations Inc.
ISBN 978-0-9939648-6-2
ASIN 0993964862

Book Cover: LWL PUBLISHING HOUSE
Inside Layout: LWL PUBLISHING HOUSE

CONTENTS

LEGAL DISCLAIMER _____ 1

FOREWORD _____ 3

DEDICATION _____ 7

ACKNOWLEDGMENTS _____ 9

INTRO AND VISION _____ 11

CHAPTER 1 _____ 13
   ANGELIC GUIDES WALK WITH ME
   BY JEWELS RAFTER

CHAPTER 2 _____ 21
   COMMUNICATING WITH YOUR ANGELIC & SPIRIT GUIDES
   BY JEWELS RAFTER

SECTION 1 _____ 35
   ANGEL SIGNS
   BY JEWELS RAFTER

CHAPTER 3 _____ 39
   CONNECTING
   BY MAUREEN SULLIVAN

ANGEL KISS _____ 43
   ANGELS OF LOVE
   BY ANU SHI ASTA

ANGEL KISS _____ 45
   INTUITION
   BY VANESSA KRICHBAUM

CHAPTER 4 ———————————————— 47
   THE GIFT OF LOVE
   BY BRIAN D. CALHOUN

ANGEL KISS ———————————————— 51
   STREET ANGEL
   BY TRACY LACROIX

ANGEL KISS ———————————————— 53
   SIGNS FROM BEYOND
   BY TRACIE MAHAN

CHAPTER 5 ———————————————— 55
SERENITY
   BY DEB BERGERSEN

ANGEL KISS ———————————————— 59
   SIGNS
   BY VANESSA KRICHBAUM

CHAPTER 6 ———————————————— 61
   DISCOVERING MY LIFE PURPOSE
   BY ANU SHI ASTA

ANGEL KISS ———————————————— 65
   HELP IS A SONG AWAY
   BY BRIAN D. CALHOUN

ANGEL KISS ———————————————— 67
   NORTH TO ALASKA
   BY ERICA JOHANSEN

CHAPTER 7 ———————————————— 69
   THE ANGEL'S GIFT
   BY DEB BERGERSEN

ANGEL KISS _____ 73
  THREE BOYS
  BY TRACIE MAHAN

ANGEL KISS _____ 75
THE LIGHT AND LOVE OF CHILDREN
  BY MAUREEN SULLIVAN

SECTION 2 _____ 79
  DIVINE COMMUNICATION
  BY JEWELS RAFTER

CHAPTER 8 _____ 83
  MANIFESTING WITH THE ARCHANGELS
  BY ANU SHI ASTA

ANGEL KISS _____ 87
  MESSAGES OF LOVE
  BY BRIAN D. CALHOUN

CHAPTER 9 _____ 89
  CALLING ON THE ANGELS
  BY TRACY LACROIX

ANGEL KISS _____ 93
  ANGELS WORK IN MYSTERIOUS WAYS
  BY JULIE DUDLEY

CHAPTER 10 _____ 95
  BETWEEN BOTH WORLDS
  BY TRACIE MAHAN

ANGEL KISS _____ 99
  LETTER TO YOUR ANGELS
  BY ANU SHI ASTA

Chapter 11 — 101
Misdiagnosed
by Gabriella Studor

Angel kiss — 105
Soul angel
by Josée Leduc

Angel kiss — 107
Forgiveness
by Tracy Lacroix

Chapter 12 — 109
Clearing essentials
by Gabriella Studor

Section 3 — 115
Healing
by Jewels Rafter

Angel kiss — 119
Archangel Jophiel
by Kimla Dodds

Angel kiss — 121
Angel of passing
by Wendy James

Chapter 13 — 123
Angels don't do stubborn
by Roni Campbell

Angel kiss — 127
A divine prescription
by Brian D. Calhoun

ANGEL KISS 129
  SURRENDERING TO THE FLOW
  BY CHRISTINE GILMOUR

CHAPTER 14 131
  HEALING MIRACLES WITH THE ANGELS
  BY MICHELE HANSON O'REGGIO

ANGEL KISS 135
  MAKING SENSE OF LIFE
  BY BARBARA GRACE REYNOLDS

CHAPTER 15 137
  INSPIRATIONS
  BY JENNIFER DEL VILLAR

SECTION 4 143
  DIVINE INTERVENTION
  BY JEWELS RAFTER

ANGEL KISS 147
  DO YOU BELIEVE IN ANGELS?
  BY DEB BERGERSEN

ANGEL KISS 149
  FALLING ANGEL
  BY MAUREEN SULLIVAN

CHAPTER 16 151
  THE POWER OF ARCHANGEL MICHAEL
  BY KIMLA DODDS

ANGEL KISS 155
  DO ANGELS INTERVENE?
  BY DEB BERGERSEN

Angel kiss ———————————————————— 157
  Crockpot story
  by Helen Cline

Chapter 17 ———————————————————— 159
  In the Arms of Angels
  by Josée Leduc

Angel kiss ———————————————————— 163
  Angel messages in my dreams
  by Deb Bergersen

Chapter 18 ———————————————————— 165
  Angel protection
  by Kimla Dodds

Section 5 ———————————————————— 173
  Channeled messages
  by Jewels Rafter

Angel kiss ———————————————————— 177
  Angel's kiss
  by Jennifer Del Villar

Chapter 19 ———————————————————— 179
  Love Is always the answer
  by Barbara Grace Reynolds

Angel kiss ———————————————————— 183
  Land of angels
  by Erica Johansen

Angel kiss ———————————————————— 185
  Merge with the angels' meditation
  by Wendy James

Chapter 20 — 189
Message from the angels
by Tracie Mahan

Chapter 21 — 193
Channeled message living the halo life
by Brian D. Calhoun

Angel kiss — 199
Trust Is the key
by Barbara Grace Reynolds

Chapter 22 — 201
Your journey
by Barbara Grace Reynolds

Chapter 23 — 205
Channeled messages from those who see
by Jennifer Del Villar

Conclusion — 209

Co-authors Bio's and Photos — 213

Legal Disclaimer

The information and content contained within this book *Guided By The Light - Following Your Angelic Guides* does not substitute any form of professional counsel such as a Psychologist, Physician, Life Coach, Clairvoyant, Medium, Spiritual Life Coach, Reiki Healer, or Counselor. The contents and information provided does not constitute professional or legal advice in any way, shape, or form.

All chapters are written at the discretion of and with the full accountability of each writer. Anita Sechesky – Living Without Limitations Inc. or LWL PUBLISHING HOUSE is not liable or responsible for any of the specific details, descriptions or names of people, places or things, personal interpretations, stories and experiences contained within. The Publisher is not liable for any misrepresentations, false or unknown statements, actions, or judgments made by any of the contributors or their chapter contents in this book. Each contributor is responsible for their own submissions and have shared their stories in good faith to encourage others.

Any decisions you make and the outcomes thereof are entirely your own doing. Under no circumstances can you hold the Compiler, LWL PUBLISHING HOUSE, or "Anita Sechesky – Living Without Limitations Inc." liable for any actions that you take.

You agree not to hold the Compiler, LWL PUBLISHING HOUSE, or "Anita Sechesky – Living Without Limitations Inc." liable for any loss or expense incurred by you, as a result of materials, advice, coaching or mentoring offered within.

The information offered in this book is intended to be general information with respect to general life issues. Information is offered in good faith; however, you are under no obligation to use this information.

Nothing contained in this book shall be considered legal, financial, or actuarial advice.

The author or Publisher assume no liability or responsibility to actual events or stories being portrayed.

It may introduce you to what a Life Coach, Counselor, Clairvoyant, Medium, Spiritual Life Coach, Reiki Healer, Psychic, Medium, or Therapist may discuss with you at any given time during scheduled sessions. The advice contained herein is not meant to replace the Professional roles of a physician or any of these professions.

Guided By The Light

Compiled by Jewels Rafter

Foreword

Everyone wants to believe that there is hope in this life despite whatever they may be going through. We all want to know that there are answers for questions that seem impossible and hard to comprehend. Life is not always easy and often times the challenges we walk through can leave a person feeling disempowered and discouraged. The thought of there being some sort of spiritual intervention bringing hope, healing, and a little faith to even believe that things will become better if we only believe and walk in an attitude of gratitude and appreciation, is more than many could even imagine; some might even say fictional and far-fetched. There are still those who choose to remain "in the dark" when it comes to stories of Angels and Spirit Guides being a part of our everyday lives. Often times, we even forget how there has been biblical stories of Angels appearing to mankind long ago to bring warnings, encouragement, and even protection around those they revealed themselves to.

As a Registered Nurse for over eleven years, I have heard many stories from colleagues and patients over the years about Angels that have been known to bring comfort and inspiration to those who believe. I feel I was very blessed to have my own Angel experience after the loss of my first child. My daughter Jasmine Rose was full-term and born sleeping. It was a difficult time for me and I had gone through a period where it was next to impossible to even talk about it. I couldn't even pray and asked my husband and mom to pray on my behalf as my heart was filled with so much grief and anxiety. I had completely lost my self-expression to inconsolable tears and heartache as her death was so unexpected. As the weeks went by, the crying changed to fear and then to nightmares. In hindsight, I realize that I entered into a season of Post Traumatic Stress Disorder. I had no professional support, as my small hometown community did not have a support group in place, although my Physician encouraged me to start a special group for other grieving parents. My hometown had a number of families who had also suffered a similar tragedy. Obviously I was not ready at this time of my life to take on such a responsibility as I myself was also walking through this horrific ordeal. My husband dealt with his grief quietly, although he was very supportive to me.

Sometime after our daughter's burial, I started having very disturbing dreams that left me terrified and feeling even more helpless and isolated. One particular night I was sitting up in bed reading, and out of the "corner of my eye," I got glimpse of something that has completely changed my perspective on supernatural beings. I witnessed the most astounding sight – right in front of me in full view for that brief second. It was like a multidimensional experience. I saw the biggest, most beautiful, and lushest wings that were swooping down across the bedroom floor, the feathers

3

were of the hugest plumes I have ever seen. I saw arms, the biggest arms with muscles that were formed, flexed, folded across and very developed, and a strong male chest. I saw a Roman skirt with long leather pleats. I saw the leather sandals that were laced up two very strong legs. I saw the sword that was strapped across the chest and hanging to the left side of his body. The blade on the sword was huge and heavy. And then I saw the face of this Angel man. It was the face of a baby, just like a cherub, gentle and yet stern. The look on the face was serious and he was on guard at the end of my bedroom, guarding me. My world instantly shifted to understand that I was not alone. God indeed cared for me and He sent his very best to protect and watch over me, despite how fearful I may be feeling. I never did have another bad dream again, after that night.

When I heard the concept of this beautiful Vision from Jewels Rafter, I knew it was a book that had to be written and that I needed to Publish. I am thankful for her vision because it will bring hope to so many people who may or may not believe in Angels and Spirit Guides. I choose to believe.

The stories you are about to read are shared because someone needs to read them. Someone needs to know the signs the look for. Someone needs to be open to the communication from their Angels. Someone needs to be in tune to hear what their Angels are saying. Someone needs to understand why clearing negativity is important. Someone needs a confirmation. Someone needs to have hope. Someone needs to walk in forgiveness, love, and peace. I believe that in order to experience a life full of these kind of blessings and a life full of abundance, there are things we must change and shift within ourselves. This book will give you that kind of insight and perspective. It may possibly change your whole way of thinking. This may be a good thing. However, if you are someone who already knows this, then you will appreciate the courage of all the contributors sharing these deeply personal and empowering stories to bring you even more hope, healing, and encouragement.

A special thanks of appreciation and gratitude to Jewels Rafter. It has been a pleasure to have you as my VIP client. A special note of appreciation to each co-author for coming along side Jewels and sharing these stories that are being brought to light on an International level. Many blessings to you our dear readers for allowing your hearts and spirits to be open to learning and understanding the significance and possibilities that await you, if you believe.

Anita Sechesky RN CPC Publisher

Compiled by Jewels Rafter

Anita Sechesky is a Best-Seller Publisher, Registered Nurse, Certified Professional Coach, NLP and LOA Wealth Practitioner, Best-Seller Consultant, multiple International Best-Selling Author, as well as a Workshop Facilitator and Conference Host. She is the Founder and CEO of Anita Sechesky - Living Without Limitations Inc. and the Founder and Publisher of LWL PUBLISHING HOUSE. Anita was born in Guyana, South America and moved to Canada when she was only four years old. Assisting many people to break through their own limiting beliefs in life and business, Anita had discovered her passion to help individuals release their stories into successful publications. She has six Best-Selling books, which includes five anthologies, encompassing approximately Two Hundred and Twenty International co-authors, who have benefited to date from her expertise. Anita launched her first solo book *"Absolutely You – Overcome False Limitations and Reach Your Full Potential"* in November 2014. As a Best-Seller Publisher, Anita helps people to put their positive perspectives into print.

To begin your exciting journey as a VIP Compiler™ with Anita on your own anthology book, or to learn more about becoming an author or co-author with LWL PUBLISHING HOUSE in one of our many anthologies, email: **lwlclienthelp@gmail.com**

Join my Private Facebook group: LIVING WITHOUT LIMITATIONS LIFESTYLE – With exclusive prizes, co-authoring opportunities and Random Contests with FREE Publishing opportunities. *Empowerment Webinar classes and more - **http://bit.ly/1TlsTSm**

Book Facebook Fan page: **http://bit.ly/211XffM**

Facebook: **www.facebook.com/AnitaSechesky/**

Email: **lwlclienthelp@gmail.com**

YouTube Channel: **http://bit.ly/1VEGHew**

Website: **www.anitasechesky.com**

LinkedIn: **https://ca.linkedin.com/in/asechesky**

Twitter: **https://twitter.com/nursie4u**

Compiled by Jewels Rafter

DEDICATION

This book is dedicated to all those who have been touched or guided by the beautiful loving light of Angelic Guides. May it confirm your belief in Angels and instill faith that you are unconditionally loved, guided, and protected from above today, tomorrow, and always...

Guided By The Light

ACKNOWLEDGMENTS

There are many people who have inspired, supported, challenged, and made me feel like I could overcome any obstacle that arose throughout my life journey; and to all these people, I am forever grateful. I felt it was necessary to acknowledge and show my gratitude for the large or small part these lovely beings have played in my life.

To my children Courtney and Breanna...thank you for being my reason to live. Thank you for loving me unconditionally throughout all the challenges and obstacles we've faced together. Because of your beautiful spirits, I have the strength to try my very best each and every day. I love you both with all my heart and soul. Hugs and kisses.

To my mother Sheila...thank you for supporting me even when you didn't understand my choices or decisions along my life journey. Thank you for always helping me find the strength and courage to move on when all I wanted to do was give up. Love you tons. Hugs and kisses.

To my father Roger...thank you for watching over me from the other side. I know you would have been proud of me for being authentically myself and for sharing my insights with the world. I miss your presence but I know you are always close by in spirit.

To Shawn...I am forever grateful for the encouragement, the continuous support, and the unconditional affection and warmth you have always shown me. You are living proof that genuine, good people still exist in a world that can be filled with so much uncertainty. Thank you for inspiring me to be the best version of myself each and every day.

To Angie...my soul sister across the pond. I love you for all those times you have been my rock, my best friend, and my confidant from near or far. I don't know how I would have gotten through all the challenges without my own personal cheering section screaming, *"I believe in you!"* You are the sister I never had and there are no words that could tell you how much your friendship means to me.

To Nathalie...thank you for being my partner in crime, my soul sister, my friend for decades. You have taught me to believe in my own magic and to be inspired by my dreams. For that, I am forever grateful and thank you eternally.

To Vanessa...I am so grateful to have connected with another version of myself in this lifetime! I knew we would be close friends from the very first time we met. Thank you for riding the roller coaster of life with me and screaming at the top of your lungs, *"Wooohoooo!"* as we welcome new adventures. You are a true gem!

To Tracie and Kimla…thank you for being the best co-hosts on Harmony Radio and now co-authors in my book! I was so touched that you agreed to be a part of this project. I love you both tons!

To Anita…thank you for believing in my book vision and for helping me to stay focused and grounded when I wanted to scream. You are a beautiful spirit who helps to uplift people and encourages them to step outside their comfort zone. I am also grateful for all the discussions about health and healing. It has helped me heal from deep within.

To my extended family…my sister-in-law Cathy, my brother Mike, my numerous cousins, my aunts, my niece, and nephew, thank you for your ongoing support and encouragement along my writer's journey. I have immense love and admiration for each and every one of you in this clan.

To my fabulous co-authors…thank you for sharing your insights, messages, and teachings with the world. I am blessed to have all of your chapters as part of this beautiful compilation. I am grateful for your ongoing support which has made this experience a very rewarding one!

To my clients, my listeners, my followers, and my friends…thank you for believing in me and for all your support from near or far. You have each touched my life in different ways.

Last but not least, I am grateful to my guardian Angels and my Spirit Guides who have helped me along this path of awakening and enlightenment. I have always felt you by my side and I thank the Universe for your guidance which enables me to help others with my gifts and abilities.

Love and light sent to all,

Jewels

Compiled by Jewels Rafter

INTRO AND VISION

"Guided by the Light – Following Your Angelic Guides" is a compilation of insights, channeled messages, and Angelic experiences told by intuitives, healers, light workers, and everyday people. As a clairvoyant and medium, I have been blessed with the opportunity to connect with my Angelic Guides on a daily basis. Yet I was wholeheartedly aware that numerous others have witnessed and felt this ethereal guidance and healing at some point in their lives. This sparked a desire to bring together a variety of people having similar experiences with Angels and Spirit Guides and share their divine stories with the world. The vision for the book derived from my desire to inspire and uplift readers as we share the beauty, unconditional love, and healing these Divine beings provide to humanity. *"Guided by the Light"* focuses on various Angel and Spirit Guide themes such as Angel Signs, Divine Communication, Healing, Divine Intervention, and Channeled Messages.

Under the *"Angel Signs"* theme, we will look at how our Angels communicate by way of subtle signs, symbols, feathers, and dreams to confirm that they are guiding and watching over us. So many people miss out on the synchronicities because they are too wrapped up in everyday life. This section will provide insights on Angelic signs and guidance all around us. We will also look at how Angels have touched and transformed people from deep within by way of undisputable signs. We have all experienced an occasion in our lives where synchronicity has occurred, feathers have been found, or messages have been received from our Angelic or Spirit Guides. It happens every day to many people and in their different walks of life. No matter what nationality, background, or social status you identify with, we have all had a divine experience at one occasion or another.

The *"Divine Communication"* theme focuses on how we connect and communicate with Angels and Spirit Guides, how we hear their messages, and how to decipher their guidance clearly and without doubt. This section contains stories about how Angels can inspire you to become a better person or how they have guided people to help others in ways they never would have. We will also look at steps you can take to communicate with your own Angel and Spirit Guides with ease and simplicity.

Under the *"Healing"* section we will share stories of emotional and spiritual healing which have occurred following Angelic signs or synchronicities. We will also look at how they have the ability to share their light and guide us towards complete health and happiness. Another focus in this section is how these Angelic Beings appear around the terminally ill and how they guide them into the light peacefully with unconditional love and support.

The *"Divine Interventions"* section will focus on miraculous stories of protection and unexplainable occurrences leading people to safety. Have Angels or Spirit Guides intervened and saved you from life-threatening or life-altering situations? This section will focus on their ability to appear when humans are in danger only to disappear moments later. The after effects of divine intervention remain with us for years and sometimes remain engrained in our spirit for the rest of our lives.

The last section entitled *"Channeled Messages"* is a beautiful compilation of inspirational and uplifting messages channeled by our intuitives and light workers. Their connection with Spirit serves as a direct conduit to the Angelic Realms as their messages bring forth inspirational guidance and direction from the Angels to be shared with all who read this compilation. Automatic writing, prophetic dreams, and channeled messages from the Light will be discussed in this section. The messages and letters are nothing less than uplifting, motivating, and full of unconditional love and acceptance.

We are in an era of spiritual awakening and ascension bringing forth higher vibrations to our planet. *"Guided by the Light – Following Your Angelic Guides"* aims to share the beauty and unconditional love that our Angelic Guides offer us if we are open and willing to listen to their guidance and messages. I hope you enjoy this anthology and come away inspired and blissful after connecting with your own Angelic Guides.

Sending each and every one of you tons of love, light, and blessings….

Jewels xx

Chapter 1

Angelic guides walk with me

Jewels Rafter

My first memory of Angels and their beautiful sparkling light occurred as I lay in my bed when I was about five years old. I recall awakening out of my slumber only to sense a radiating warmth in the room. An iridescent sparkling light brightened up the corner of my bedroom and I felt safe, calm, and content to watch it sparkle. This light seemed to gradually grow and fill up half of my bedroom with its luminescence. As it grew and sparkled, I felt the need to reach out and touch the light with my fingertips.

Like a toddler reaching towards a parent to be lifted up, I outstretched my arms towards the ceiling only to hear a musical laughter as my fingers connected with this light. I remember giggling to myself and thinking that this light was magic of some sort. As the laughter left my lips, I felt a wave of warmth wrap around my shoulders like someone holding me in their arms. This warmth radiated an intense feeling of love made me close my eyes and smile. I heard a far off voice whisper, *"I am always here to watch over you, little one. Go to sleep."*

At a young age, I was aware of their presence and vowed to stay connected with this loving, healing energy going forward. Little did I know that these Divine Beings would become a very big part of my life, both in my personal relationships as well as in my career! As a professional clairvoyant and medium, I have always been directed by my Angelic and Spirit guides. I have been blessed enough to experience their beautiful light, experienced their unconditional love, and heard their uplifting messages which allowed me to help others find guidance and support. Fortunately, these Angelic beings are not exclusive to only intuitive people like myself! They are accessible to everyone and anyone who asks for their help and guidance. They are tuned into your energy and can sense when you are in a life-threatening situation, but otherwise they will not interfere with your life unless you ask them to help or guide you. In my work as a spiritual teacher and energy healer, I often call upon angels as guides to assist in energy healing sessions; they are such powerful natural healers. You'll definitely want to learn how to contact your angels so you can call them to your side to heal, support, guide, or simply inspire you.

How can we be certain that they are not a figment of our imagination or a result of an overactive mind? Why are these beings present in our lives and why do they watch over us? Belief in Angels has formed part of humanity's spiritual quest down through the ages, and references to Angels can be found in every religion, every culture, and every century. Angels have been discussed and believed in for many centuries. The ideology of Angelic presence can be found in literature, religious manuals, and paintings throughout diverse cultures around the world. But what exactly are these creatures?

The Angelic Kingdom is said to have been created as part of an earlier evolution of this Universe. Angels are perceived as Divine Beings of light whose purpose it is to anchor Divinity on Earth. They emanate from a stream of consciousness outside of the dimensions known to humans, from the dimension of original Divine Source and Spirit. They are divine messengers, guides and teachers able to transcend time and space as we know it. It is said that Angels work on the golden ray of true unconditional love and wisdom, and certainly, Angels have immeasurable love and compassion for us and for our planet as we work through these times of huge turbulence and change which are causing us so much distress on many levels.

Angels are literally made of love and light; basically they are made of energy. They can choose to take human or any other form, but their true natural state of being is as radiant white light and as untainted, unconditional love. They have never been human, yet they still have a consciousness; they are thinking, individual beings with their own personalities, but they do not have a body. Their consistency is the very mechanism we use as the healing agent in energy medicine: pure positive energy! This means that all Angels have the ability to energetically heal you instantaneously, no matter what type of healing you need. And trust me, they are among the most powerful energy healers you can find! Angels embody the Divine, and when the highest vibration of Divine Love is anchored into your own consciousness through a down pouring of pure energy, you have the ability to change your reality and heal physically, mentally, and spiritually.

These beauties do not harness any negativity as they are a conduit to divine love, the most powerful love in the Universe. These loving souls come from the radiant connection of Source and Spirit. Can you imagine just how peaceful it must be to live in that kind of pure energy? These ethereal beings bring that divine love back down to Earth to share with you, so that you can also experience the life-changing unconditional acceptance. Once you have felt the warmth and complete bliss of their energy, your consciousness expands, and you become more self-aware, more conscious of the love all around you. This is why that feeling of peace, warmth, or unconditional love usually follows an experience with Angelic beings.

Although they surround us and watch over people on earth, they are not permitted to intervene or alter any of your life choices. Therefore, in order for Angels to communicate, guide, or assist you, it is essential to ask them for assistance. It does occur during times of grief or sadness that these loving souls will provide signs of their existence like leaving a small white feather in your vicinity. This is simply a message that they are watching over you during your hardship. Subsequently, in order to get the most out of your relationship with your Angels (as with any relationship), communication is the key.

In my teenage years, I truly began to develop my intuition and clairvoyant abilities and it was at that point in time I felt the presence of both my Angels and my Spirit guide, which I named Jacob. Both energies are loving and very supportive beings, however, they are two very separate entities. This I learned along my intuitive journey and spiritual awakening. When my Angels were present, the energy in the room would consist of a very pure caliber and high vibration. A sensation of goosebumps covered by body as the room filled up with light, peaceful energy, and warmth. A sudden calmness would wash over me and instantaneously, I felt safe and loved. This is how I knew my Angels were near. They would also provide signs such as random feathers on the floor, reoccurring numbers on the clock or even the sound of bell chimes in the distance when I was too busy to notice their presence. At times, as a teenager, I was oblivious to the most incredible occurrences, however, when Angels were near I felt the energy shift around me right away.

When my Spirit guide Jacob would appear, I felt a presence to my right side, as though a person may have been standing next to me. I could practically see him from the corner of my eye, yet each time I turned my head in that direction, frustratingly, he disappeared. With time and practice, I had the ability to hear and see him around me. Since early childhood I have been a medium, which means I have the ability to connect with passed loved ones and communicate with them whilst they are in spirit. Meditation and slowing down my thoughts aided me in hearing and seeing Jacob. This is why communicating with my Guide became second nature and effortless. Spirit Guides have usually existed in human form at one point in their lives. Angels, on the other hand, have not. When people pass into the light and go to the other side (or Heaven as some may call it), they have the opportunity to become a Guide and choose a human here on earth to support and help along that individual's life journey. They're responsible for helping us fulfill the spiritual contract we make with ourselves before we are born. Spirit Guides choose to assist us and serve as a connection to the Spirit World. These celestial beings are non-judgmental and have an abundance of compassion, which helps when dealing with stubborn creatures like ourselves! They have been referred to as our sixth sense or even that voice inside your head that tells you to move forward or to pull back in any given situation.

Spirit Guides are allocated to one person in particular on the earth plane, whereas Angels or Angelic Guides are here to enlighten, transform, and protect humanity as a whole. Angels' goal is to shift the negativity on earth into positivity, peace, unconditional love, and acceptance for all on the planet. They wish to help us transition with hope, joy, and become in tune with the new energy present on earth. There is a spiritual awakening happening all over the planet thanks to these divine beings.

Furthermore, Angels have the ability to assist us in life or death situations, this is called Divine Intervention. Otherwise, they do not intervene in your personal choices, relationships, or life journey. When a critical situation such as a car accident, injury, or traumatic event occurs, Angels can however intervene and save us. This is the only instance that they will assist humans without requesting their help. You can ask for help with anything from taking a test, finding a parking place, meeting the perfect mate, or even healing cancer or disease.

Being a holistic therapist and energy worker, I always call upon my Angelic Healing Guides to help me during a reiki and energy balancing session with clients. The healing energy is channeled from the Angelic Realms by my Healing Angels and I am simply the conduit which directs this pure loving energy to those in need of healing. With their guidance, I am able to channel their loving, healing vibrations which helps to speed up emotional and physical healing.

In 2007 while living in Europe, I was blessed with opportunity to learn Angelic Reiki. I was already a Reiki Master and felt I needed to acquire some new healing modalities. Angelic Reiki's energy is a pure Angelic vibration which is beautiful, gentle, and resonates at a much higher frequency than other healing modalities. It is the healing power of all the Masters of other Reiki lineages combined with the Angelic Vibration, through Archangel Metatron, to create Angelic Reiki. I researched further and learned that his modality also used symbols common to other Reiki systems, however the Divine vibration which flows and attunes both healer and client to their Soul energy, gives Angelic Reiki that something extra. Therefore I decided it was a perfect fit for me. This life-changing experience touched my inner spirit and to this day, the Angelic journey remains engrained in my mind. My connection with the Angelic realms has deepened tremendously and I am deeply moved by and in awe of the magnificence of the experience of becoming one with these pure, loving creatures from the heavens.

During the course, our teacher explained that we would be learning how to connect with the Archangels and other divine beings. We would also journey, by way of a guided meditation, and visit the Kingdom of Light. This location, she explained, was the heavenly realm where the Angels resided. Although I had experienced the presence of my Spirit Guide Jacob many times and felt the loving energy of Angels in the past, I found it quite difficult to imagine a journey to the heavens! Little did I know that this divine experience would connect me directly with the light and send my clairvoyant and healing abilities through the roof! As a group, we were taught the symbols and frequencies needed to connect with the Angelic realm and the blissful energy in the room began to vibrate. During training, the initiations and attunements allowed the highest vibration of love to anchor into our hearts and souls with irreversible, profound effects. As we raised our vibrations by way of positive thoughts and asked the Angels to be present with us, chills permeated through me and touched my soul. I felt unconditional love for myself, for all those in the room and for all that walked the earth and heavens. Moments later, the Angels stood among us! I forgot where I was and simply focused on the beautiful vibrations of love that filled that small room. As I shifted my attention to the feelings washing over me, I heard my teacher's voice in the background encouraging us to open our hearts further and follow the Angelic beings into the Kingdom of light.

I felt myself falling deep into meditation, yet simultaneously moving forward. In my mind's eye I saw a doorway appear that slowly opened and shone with a brilliant iridescent light. I walked towards the door and as I got closer, I heard the sounds of chimes and the most melodic ethereal singing coming from the other side of it. I stepped through the doorway knew right away I had walked into a completely different dimension on the Spirit plane. The sky was a beautiful color of turquoise and violet, and a white building in the form of an amphitheatre stood before me. Hundreds of white steps filled the space and spiraled up to a glowing pointed arch at the top. The stairs were filled with Angels of all shapes, sizes, and colors. The room seemed to contain thousands of the beautiful creatures of light glowing and sending unconditional love my way. I felt like my heart would explode at any moment. The sensations were so intense, yet I did not want it to stop. Shivers covered my entire body and my soul felt like it was vibrating to the sound of their Angelic voices as they sang. At the very arch of the building stood the most immense impressive beings. I knew instinctively that they were the Archangels.

I heard a resounding voice that said, *"I am Metatron my dear one, I am here to welcome you to our Kingdom of love and healing. We are always with you and surround you with love and light."* Being so tall, it was impossible for me to discern his face. His glowing hands were positioned just above the archway and were radiating golden light onto me. A bolt of energy ran through my spine as he put his hand on the crown of my head sending vibrations of unconditional love. I felt as though I was literally flying and my perception was heightened to levels I never knew I could achieve! I was communicating with other dimensions! And the deep personal healing I was experiencing was massive. The center of the arch glowed brighter with a radiant white light and the most beautiful tones rang in my ears. I have never heard a sound so pure and so mesmerizing to this very day. For what seemed like both an instant and an eternity, I basked in the feelings of peace and love like I had never experienced before. The sound of my teacher's voice guiding us back to reality awoke me from my meditative state. Instantly I was back in my physical body in the room with everyone else.

I opened my eyes and tears of joy streamed down my face. I felt as though I had been floating on air riding a soft cloud of happiness and serenity. Everyone around the room observed each other with a look of awe and contentment. I felt such gratitude for the experience that allowed me to connect with the Divine and with Angels. I knew at that moment, that I could always call upon these Divine beings whenever I desired.

As I returned home, the experience played in my mind over and over. Each time I felt the presence of my Angels right there beside me. As the weeks flew by, my clairvoyant abilities began to develop further. As I came into contact with others, I began to discern an energetic glow around their bodies (their auras), I could sense their physical ailments, and hear their innermost thoughts and feelings. My readings became more accurate and I no longer needed tools such as oracle cards or pendulums to connect with them. To this day, I have the ability to read people's energy and see their past, present, and future possibilities. I believe the Angels helped to propel me forward and guide me towards living my life purpose and my passion. It drove my desire to heal and assist others by means of energy healing, readings, counseling, and connecting with their loved ones on the other side. To this very day, I am guided by the light of these Divine Beings. I am beyond blessed to have this ability, and to each of my Guides and Angels, I remain forever grateful.

We all have Angels and Spirit Guides by our side watching over us and waiting for the day where we will reach out to them for assistance. Spirit is always waiting to help and heal you when you are in need. Conscious contact with your higher power can be achieved through meditation, prayer, patience, and the innermost desire to communicate with these Divine Beings. Speak to them, listen, and watch for signs of their presence. As long as you keep in conscious contact with your higher power, be assured that you will be guided on the right path and protected from harm. Remember to be conscious of your surroundings, and keep your eyes opened for random white feathers...a sure sign they are watching over you, dear soul.

Chapter 2

Communicating with your Angelic & Spirit Guides

Jewels Rafter

This chapter will give you the tools to connect with your Angelic and Spirit Guides. By the end of the sections, you should be on your way to creating abundance, love, and happiness with the help of your own Guides! We all have Guardian Angels and Spirit Guides whether we realize it or not. The spirit world is all around us and in reality we all exist in different dimensions. You see, most people go through their lives with only a limited awareness of spirit, but the good news is that learning to communicate with these beautiful beings is easier than you may realize. All that is required is for you to have an open heart and mind to the whole experience.

HOW DO WE KNOW THEY ARE REALLY THERE?

One of the common questions asked is how do we really know they are there and that isn't our imagination working overtime? One of the signs that spirit is around is that we see glimpses from the corner of our eye of a shadow or form. Other signs are experiencing coincidences quite frequently, repetitive numbers, doors opening by themselves, feathers found indoors, a soft knocking sound when no one else is home, and flickering lights. All of these are signs of the seen and unseen dimensions.

SO WHO CAN COMMUNICATE WITH SPIRIT?

Some people are born with the innate ability to sense spirit, far more clearly than most, like myself. This ability can be both a blessing and a curse as it occurs often automatically without notice. However, it is possible for anybody to learn the techniques required to communicate efficiently with their Spirit Guides and Angels. When working with the spirit world, I always urge you to do so with absolute respect and positive intentions. Learning to work with your Spirit Guides is a slow process and can take time to master, so be patient with yourself! Getting impatient or frustrated will only delay clear communication further.

OUR PERSONAL SPIRIT GUIDES

Firstly, everyone is blessed with a Spirit Guide devoted to you. However, don't expect Elvis or Einstein to show up on your first encounter. Many hope to have a spiritual connection with a great figure from history, but usually your Spirit Guide is not these famous people. We chose our Guides before incarnating here on earth, and our higher selves always choses the right guide for your life path. Throughout our life journey, we usually are graced with and have numerous Guides. Some are with us for a specific reason or situation we may be going through and some are by our side for a lifetime, like my own Spirit Guide Jacob.

TYPES OF GUIDES

Ascended Masters

These are Guides who have led many reincarnated lives here on earth and gradually evolved to a higher level of consciousness, enlightenment and awareness. We are all on the same journey - including the Ascended Masters. These spirits have simply chosen to help us on our journey. I like to call these beings the celebrities of the spirit world. They usually don't work with only one soul but focus on helping humanity as a whole. In early stages of connecting with Spirit Guides, it's highly unlikely that you will connect with these enlightened beings. However, the longer you practice speaking with the spirit world, the more likely that you will eventually come to meet these celebs! Examples of these celebs would be Jesus, Buddha, or Krishna.

Angelic Guides

These Divine Beings are made of pure light, unconditional love, and they herald messages of enlightenment, hope, and peace. They usually appear when you are in need of healing or in a situation where you feel completely distraught or consumed with grief. Angelic Guides wish to uplift and heal you and are non-judgmental and completely accepting of any situation you may be faced with. In order to communicate with them, it is crucial to be in a state of calmness and openness. These celestial creatures are accessible to everyone and anyone who asks for their help and guidance.

Ancestors & Family

Ancestor worship is extremely common across most cultures and even in modern times, we still remember our passed family members and pay homage to them when times are challenging. So it's not surprising that working with these Guides is like a family affair. Our Ancestors are part of our bloodlines. Recently deceased relatives often show up as Guides, as well as distant relatives who passed centuries ago. In most cases, it is the spirit of our ancestors both recent and ancient who we encounter when we first start communicating with spirit. These Guides are most protective and helpful and offer the best guidance and advice because they have our best interest at heart.

Archetypes

These Guides usually have a theme or a persona and are easily recognizable. For example they may be a healer, a warrior, a priest, a shaman, a monk, a teacher, a medicine doctor, and many more. They appear at a specific point in our lives where we need guidance. They help with a specific path we must travel or they are present to teach life lessons, or even intercede on our behalves. Archetypes are similar to patron saints. They guide with great depth of insight, knowledge, and power during difficult and dark times. When you encounter these beings it is crucial and very important to take note of their messages or guidance. They usually appear when there is a real need and should not be ignored.

Animal Guides

In the spirit world, relationships between humans and non-humans are interwoven. As we all have spirits, we are connected. Native Americans understood this link and recognized it by building totems and shamanic traditions. Other cultures throughout history have also identified themselves with different traits and spirits of animals like the Egyptians or most of the Orient. In the spirit world, animals are also present without earth based traits like aggression. Many people will discover that at least one of their main Guides is an animal. These Guides appear to teach a life lesson rather than offer guidance. Many animal Guides provide protection in both spirit and the manifested world. Treat them with respect, love, and affection. As they can be amongst the most companionable and protective spirits. A sign that you have an animal guide is seeing this animal repetitively in many areas of your life. Perhaps an animal you see in a reoccurring commercial, or an animal that crosses your path daily, or seeing that post on Facebook with the same specific animal.

PATIENCE

Your Spirit Guides are very much on your side and they are there to help you achieve your goals, learn your life lessons, and live your life's purpose. So remember that learning to work with them is a slow process which takes time and patience. It is a slow step-by-step process that flows based on absolute trust. So take the time it needs to master this process; be patient with yourself because getting frustrated will not help, on the contrary, it will slow you down.

CREATING THE RIGHT ATMOSPHERE

When creating any great relationship, it is essential to offer the right environment in order to communicate effectively. When communicating with the spirit world, it is highly unlikely that free flowing communication occurs in a busy environment. A room filled with a radio, television, internet, or a hoard or young children is not the right place to start your attempts to connect. While experienced shamans, mediums, and healers can connect anywhere, they normally go somewhere quiet, a place of silence, or somewhere where distractions are minimized. So as a beginner it's crucial to create an environment where there are absolutely no distractions. Calm is required and is essential for smooth communication with the spirit world.

HANDY TOOLS

When creating a sacred space for communication it's essential to make it as personal and as serene as possible. Before getting started I always like to have the following items ready:

1. A comfortable space to sit or lie down.

2. Comfortable non-restrictive clothes (it's not time for that little black dress!).

3. A blanket if you have a tendency to get cold easily.

4. A candle of any color.

5. Incense if you desire - try Sandalwood for opening up communication

6. Clear quartz crystal to clear the energy in your space.

7. A pen and paper/notebook.

CASTING A CIRCLE OF PROTECTION

Casting circles has been a tradition in spiritual ceremonies for centuries. So do not worry, this is not witchcraft! At all times, we will be working with the light and in the light. We will be communicating and calling on divine beings of light, Angelic beings only. Casting a circle simply means we are creating a safe and sacred energetic space where we can welcome our Guides.

Prior to opening up the channels of communication, we must create a circle of light and energy around us. So what I usually do is I stand in the middle of the room where I am working, I take my clear quartz and point in directly in front of me. Slowly I make a circle all around me for 360 degrees. I visualize white light coming out of the end of the quartz and creating a circle of white light all around me.

As I do this I say:

"I cast this circle of protection filled with love and light. I call upon the Angelic beings of light to protect me and keep all unwanted spirits that do not have my best interest at heart. I also ask Archangel Michael to stand by my side and protect me. Thank you."

IS ANYBODY THERE AND HOW LONG IS THIS GOING TO TAKE?

Ok, so you have cast your circle, you have meditated for hours and still... nothing. No apparitions, no voices, no messages and you think you have failed. Or have you? Spirit Guides are not in the habit of making grand entrances or giving big elaborate performances. Their presence is fairly constant, but it takes time to attune yourself to their vibrations and presence. If your first attempts get no results, do not be disenchanted or upset. Spirit Guides often work on their own schedule. Just because you created a sacred space does not mean they will show up instantly. However when you create a space, time, and right atmosphere, it will encourage them to make themselves known or more apparent. It's important to remember they have always been with you, but you were not always fully aware of their presence. So the process is kind of like fine tuning a radio to get the correct station. It takes patience and the right energy to get communication flowing.

SO WHAT'S THE CATCH?

You may be asking yourself what's the key to connecting with my Angelic or Spirit Guides? What's the trick? Lucky for us, there is no trick, only one key; meditation and quieting your mind. In order to hear the messages clearly we need to be in a state of mindfulness, where you are focused clearly on the moment. It means being completely present in the now. I realize that not everybody knows how to meditate or quiet their minds. This doesn't always come easy for everyone.

A good starting place for a beginner is to try a guided meditation to get your brain used to disconnecting from everything around you. The trick is to quiet the thoughts in your mind and this comes with patience and practice, therefore don't get frustrated if a state of Zen does not happen instantly. Think of a relationship with your Guides as if it was a dance with a partner. You cannot dance as a couple in sync without the music, rhythm, or right flow of energy. Communication with your Spirit Guide happens when the energy is right and when you are both on the same vibrational level. Yes, now we are talking about energy vibrations.

A FEW NO NO's

A key element to this process is openness and willingness to forget any preconceived notions you may have about how it will go down. Try not to decide ahead of time exactly who your Guide is or will be. Be open to the possibilities of magical encounters. Another suggestion is to not put a timescale on the process. Everyone is unique and learns or proceeds at different speeds. So what takes you two weeks may take your friend three months. Avoid discussing what you are trying with negative or cynical people, as negative energy slows down the process and only makes you defensive. Alternatively, keep supportive and like-minded people around you.

ANOTHER USEFUL TOOL

One the most important tools to have when you are on this journey of discovery is a JOURNAL! They are a great way for recording progress and keeping track of messages or patterns during your meetings. Start by recording any contact you have with your Guides because most of us have more than just one Spirit Guide. Please note that when you begin this process of communication, it is highly likely that you will encounter either an Ancestor or an Animal Guide. Just be open to welcoming any guide who makes themselves known to you. As you would thank a friend or visitor, don't forget to thank them at the end of each meeting as gratitude opens the flow of communication.

Animal Guide spirits don't necessarily show up in full coherent form or apparition. A strong clue that you have made contact is seeing a specific animal repeatedly in your environment afterwards. If every time you open your FB and there is a post about a wolf, if you turn on your television and there is a documentary on wolves, then you go shopping and the lady next to you is wearing a shirt that says howl at the moon…chances are your guide is a wolf spirit! See the pattern?

Ancestor Guides let us know they are around in similar ways. You may bump into a stranger who reminds you of a relative, or they drive the same car, or seeing their name everywhere is also a sign that they are making themselves known!

HAVING THE RIGHT ENERGY VIBRATIONS

The spirit world and the earth plane both vibrate at different frequencies as we are both in different dimensions. The earth plane holds human emotions such as anger, hatred, vengeance, and jealousy - all lower vibrating energies. On the spirit plane, the vibrations are much higher as those on the other side come from a place of love and light, which vibrate at a much faster level. I like to compare it to a blender. Humans can be compared to the chop button on the blender which spins at a low speed. The spirit world, however, vibrates like the liquefy button, at a higher speed.

So in order to communicate effectively, we have to be vibrating at the same frequency. Just like a proper Wi-Fi connection; downloads take forever when the signal is weak. Whereas when the connection is at 5 bars, then poof! Downloads are almost instant! Get the picture?

TIPS & INSIGHTS FOR CLEAR COMMUNICATION

Clear communication is not an instant process with the spirit world. So when trying these steps bear in mind that it can take weeks and sometimes months before you can see your Guide completely. Do not worry however, as they eventually do appear. In the beginning, you may see them, hear them, or simply sense their presence around you. So if you sense something, say hello! Introduce yourself as you would to a new friend. I know that might sound crazy as they already know it's you, but it's still wise to introduce yourself at this point. If you recognize their energy as being a friend or relative, tell them how pleased you are to see them. If it is nobody you know, ask them politely for their name. Usually a name is the very first message you will get. If their name is not familiar to you, write it down in your journal.

For most of us, the logical next question would be, *"Do you have any messages for me?"* In many cases, the first encounter they won't have much to say. This is because the first encounter is simply an introduction. Now I am not saying it will never happen, as occasionally it does happen that they have messages. So if it does occur in the introduction meeting, write it down!! The messages are usually quite important, as your Spirit Guide is not wasting time.

Always thank your spirit Guides for any form of communication or sign they offer you. Remember that gratitude opens the door to possibilities

STEPS FOR COMMUNICATING WITH YOUR SPIRIT GUIDES

1. MEDITATE – PRACTICE quieting your mind because if you cannot quiet the thoughts, communication is going to be a challenge! Remember how hard it was to get a connection with bad Wi-Fi? Well it's the same principal. In fact, in order to make real lasting contact with your Spirit Guide, I encourage you to meditate daily to establish an initial clear connection. Even if it's only for ten minutes a day.

2. RAISE YOUR VIBRATIONS. To connect with your Guide you have to raise your vibrational frequency to the range where you can perceive them. Their energy flows on a vibration of pure love and light. So what exactly does raising vibrations mean? It means moving to a more positive emotion. Our focus must be on positive thoughts since they are the basis for higher vibrations,

whereas negative thoughts slow down our energy and weighs us down. You see, you cannot focus on things that make you feel bad and still hold a high vibration at the same time. That conversation is not going to happen. When we are in our happy place, our energy is light and vibrates faster like theirs. That is the space we need to be in order to connect efficiently.

3. BE CLEAR IN YOUR INTENTIONS. It's important to be clear about the types of spirits you want to attract. State something like, *"I invite all my own loving and wise spirit Guides to join me and to come forth in peace from the light."* Chose phrases and words you are comfortable for you to say. Clarity is essential when asking for their help. Be specific and detailed.

4. CALL ON BACKUP! If you feel you need more spiritual or Angelic protection, surround yourself in a bubble of white light and call on Archangel Michael or any other deity you resonate with to keep you safe and protected. This will ensure that you are covered on all sides.

5. CREATE YOUR CIRCLE OF PROTECTION- Prior to opening up the channels of communication, stand in the middle of the room where you are working. Hold the clear quartz in your hand, extend your arm and point it directly in front of you. Slowly make a circle all around you for 360 degrees. Visualize white light coming out of the end of the quartz and creating a circle of white light all around you.

6. GROUND YOURSELF – We often forget to ground ourselves before doing any type of energy work. A good way to do this is to close your eyes, and imagine that tree roots are coming out of soles of your feet and are sinking deep into the ground and into the earth's core. Feel it anchoring you to the earth as your energy grounds and stabilizes.

7. VISUALIZE YOUR SACRED SPACE – See a place in your mind where you feel relaxed or feel a sense of sacredness such as in nature, on the beach, by the sea, in the forest, a quiet serene place where you feel connected to spirit and the beauty around you.

8. SIT IN YOUR SACRED SPACE – Sit down in this space and take in all the sights and sounds.

9. CALL FOR THEM AND WAIT – Ask your guide to come closer and sit next to you. Ask them to show themselves.

10. INTRODUCE YOURSELF – When they arrive, introduce yourself as you would to a new acquaintance. Thank them for coming and listening to your prayers to meet with you.

11. ASK YOUR QUESTION – Ask them your questions! Don't bombard them with 500 questions, but gently ask what is on your mind

12. WAIT FOR AN ANSWER – Be patient!!! Sometimes it takes time to hear them clearly or to get an answer right away.

13. SAY GOOD BYE AND THANK YOU – Always be polite and thank them for their time. It creates a stronger relationship with them down the road!

BENEFITS

Guides help us to accomplish the purpose we have set for ourselves throughout our life journey. When we are clear and specific in what we need from them, Spirit Guides will actively furnish you with the means to achieve your desires. Consider them your teammates or partners and make it a fruitful partnership! Working with Spirit Guides creates opportunities in your life as it is an enlightening experience. Those who practice regularly become quite quick at connecting and the opportunities coming from the world of spirit is invaluable.

SIGNS YOU HAVE MADE CONTACT

If you want to know that you are talking to the right spirit, the messages received should always be positive, helpful, and should make you feel positive about yourself. A Spirit Guide will not tell you what you should do as they are Guides, not leaders. They will provide suggestions and ideas but never orders or threats and always coming from love. They will never be angry, hurtful, or scary because our Guides are supportive and loving.

Keep an eye out for repetition in your life with regards to images, words, symbols, or numbers because these are signs that we are making contact and they are trying to make contact. Synchronicities are also a sign that they are near and working their magic. They like to use this technique to get your attention. They figure that if they keep aligning meaningful coincidences over and over again, then maybe you will clue in!

I wish you luck and success in your communication adventures with spirit! Once you start doing it on a regular basis, you will see your life change in many positive ways. This is the beginning of a beautiful relationship with the spirit plane, so make the most of it and enjoy the guidance and healing this experience will bring.

Compiled by Jewels Rafter

SECTION 1
ANGEL SIGNS

SECTION 1

Angel signs

Jewels Rafter

Angels leave signs to reassure, comfort, and guide us. These signs may simply signify that they are present, that they have answers to our questions, or wish to offer guidance to help us through difficult times. Often, these signs appear in unexpected places and times. In order to distinguish them, we must be open and attentive to the subtle signs. Awareness is the key! The spirit world communicates with us continuously, however it is our responsibility to be attentive and listen. The Angels send us messages on license plates, repeated songs on the radio, intuitive feelings, and Divine Timing occurrences or sometimes through other individuals. Some may call these events synchronicity or coincidence. However if you truly believe that everything happens for a reason, there can be no coincidence. These are your Angelic and Spirit Guides speaking to you. When you become aware of the signs and listen to their messages, your life flows and everything around you falls into place.

The universe responds to our inner yearnings by mysteriously bringing people into our life to answer our questions and help quell our conflicts. Every time you follow your intuition, your personal vibration intensifies. This can be compared to connecting to a strong Wi-Fi signal in a public location. The more your personal vibration is intensified the more you will attract Angels and people into your life who carry messages for you. It is the universal law of attraction.

You see, your Angels will never send you a neon flashing sign which screams *"We Are Here!"* Instead, you are more likely find a feather or a dime on the floor, notice synchronicities or reoccurring numbers on clocks or phones or even hear your name called in a soft voice when you are alone. These are some of the ways Angelic Guides like to signify their presence. There are many Angels surrounding each one of us all the time, offering love, support, and guidance. All we need do is be still enough to listen (with all of our senses) and we will know they are close by. The key is to listen with all of your senses for a sign. They are always present, but you must raise your "antennas" to recognize them.

Angels can communicate with you in various ways. You may be prompted to watch a specific television program, read a book, go on a journey, or spend time with specific people. White feathers often appear once you start to expand your awareness to these Divine beings of energy and light. You may get a sense of inner knowing and feel compelled to follow up on a message or sign without reason. You may also start to see energies moving around you through the corner of your eye. They will resemble tiny sparkles of light or sparks. These are usually your Spirit Guides or Angels hovering close by. You may also notice a shimmering iridescent light, that kind of looks like those heat waves that appear on roads in the summertime.

Angel signs are transpiring whether you acknowledge them or not! They may leave dimes on the floor, cause the lights in the room to flicker, create sparkles of light which you may see from the corner of your eye, or even make the volume on electronic devices fluctuate up and down! The Angels whisper through synchronicities to get your attention. They can also create physical symptoms on humans such as experiencing goosebumps or shivers from head to toe followed by a feeling of warmth or coldness. Another interesting technique they use is showing you reoccurring numbers on your clock, or digital devices. It is not a coincidence to see 11:11, 2:22, or 3:33 etc., on the clock when they are sending signs in your direction. Or perhaps you are driving and keep seeing the same number repetitively on license plates! For example, you turn on the car and the time on the clock says 1:11 pm. Then you start your journey and the license plate on the car in front of you has the numbers 111 on it. Stepping into the grocery store and the total for your order is $11.11! Coincidence, I think not! This, again, is a sign of their presence.

By thinking kind and positive thoughts, you will strengthen your aura and emit a higher vibration which attracts these celestial beings more rapidly. Angels are attracted to loving and peaceful energies. Therefore, if you are hoping to see signs of their presence, it is crucial to be in a place of love and light as much as possible. Being in a place of gratitude and acceptance also helps to bring them closer to you.

Children and infants are very blessed as they can easily see and interact with their Angels as they have no preconceptions or biased beliefs. They see them as clear as daylight. This reality became very evident one day during a session with one of my clients. She came to me for a clairvoyant reading and for some guidance on how to move forward after the difficult passing of her mother.

As we sat down and started our session, her three-year-old daughter sat quietly on the floor next to her mother playing with her crayons and coloring book. This beautiful woman was very distraught as she did not sense her mother's energy around her since her passing. As tears welled up in her eyes, she confided that she felt very alone and riddled with grief on a daily basis. Her daughter kept looking up at her mother and focused on something behind her head. Each time she lifted her face, she smiled at her mother and giggled to herself.

I explained to my client that sometimes when we are overcome with heavy emotions such as grief and sadness, it is very difficult to sense spirit around us as the energy of these emotions vibrates at a much slower rate than positive feelings. Tears streamed down her face and she admitted having dark thoughts most of the time and feeling as though she was completely alone. She was overwhelmed with grief and began to sob. Her daughter once again lifted her head from her masterpiece, and smiled and laughed at something behind my client. The mother leaned towards her daughter and asked her gently what she was smiling and laughing at?

The child broke into a giggle and said, *"Mommy don't you see the sparkling Angel lady standing behind you? She is right next to you. See, you're not alone, silly Mommy!"* Out of the mouths of babes comes the truth. This unbiased child could see her mother's Angel as clear as she saw us both sitting before her. She felt the loving energy and saw the light that emanated from this celestial being which enabled her to connect so easily. It was a beautiful reminder that in order to see or hear the Angels around us, it is imperative to be in a state of awe and acceptance similar to that of a small child. Being positive and in a state of grace and gratitude is the key to attracting these beautiful, loving beings into your life.

It is very acceptable to ask your Guides or Angels to provide you with signs of their presence. Request that they deliver clear, concise signs that they are near.

I promise you will be surprised just how fast symbols appear.

Chapter 3

Connecting

Maureen Sullivan

My sister's cottage in gorgeous Renfrew County, Ontario, has always held the most peaceful and spiritual energy for me. As someone who connects with the elementals, the gentle sound of the lake water rippling in the sun, the canopy of trees, and the silence you can hear in amongst the various fairy doors and portals, I am always at home.

At many times in my life, I have felt the guidance and support of what I have come to believe as my Angelic or Spirit Guides. This has occurred most often when I have been in painful depths within myself or external life situations, such as my violent relationship, which I felt trapped in, or at times when I have felt different in this world. I have often been energetically supported by the unseen. They connect with me as a knowing to remind me. Twice at this beautiful sanctuary with my mother and sister, I experienced them and their power in a very different way. In human form, as an Earth Angel, and as an energy I recognized.

The first time, in 2012, my mother and sister had arrived in the village of Eganville to shop before heading out to the cottage. We were in the store and I was drawn to this man with snow white long hair who flitted about the grocery store with such a lightness, my eyes were mesmerized by him. My sister who was walking with me, also noticed this presence. We soon became conscious of the fact that we were staring! I felt as though I was oblivious to my surroundings and that everything in the store faded before me and around me. I was drawn to this person, as I shared with my sister, energetically. There was an aura of light that I was curious about. I felt full of wonder and full of love. For no reason, yet every reason, my sister and I clung onto each other's arms as we consciously followed on the path this man was leading us on.

When we arrived at the cash register, my mother who had walked ahead, asked if we noticed the white-haired man. My sister and I were somehow not surprised by her noticing him and asking us. It was as if he was put in our path for our eyes only. As the white-haired man left the store, he turned to the three of us and smiled a gleaming smile through the window of the store. His gaze looked through everything and glared into what felt like something at a soul level. When we got in the car for the ride back to the cottage, we sat in silence with a shared knowingness that for reasons unknown, we had just had a collective experience. He, by all intents and purposes, was just a man. A human being. But why had we all felt this strange connection with him and between us. I felt full of my own light, this stranger's light, my sister's light, and my mother's light. All joined and connected in ways that defy logic. But we felt it.

We chatted about this experience when we got back to the cottage and as my mother and sister took a nap, I sat outside on the dock and felt surrounded by a light unexplained. I had my Angel oracle cards with me and had been looking at the Archangel Michael card which I pulled. I personally felt His strength and protective light around me while sitting on the dock alone. I smiled, again with the validation of what I felt. We were protected. We were loved. We were connected.

When they awoke, they both had commented with emotion how touched they were by this presence and how he had been in their dreams as a spiritual presence. I exclaimed to them that I truly believed that this presence was Angelic and felt like the energy of Archangel Michael. His embodiment in human form. Protector and guardian. There was this moment, sitting on the dock, where in love and emotion, the three of us were joined by this amazing experience of pure love. In that very moment, a male voice from somewhere across the lake, began to sing the song "The Rose" in the most beautiful operatic male voice. Almost as if he had wanted to share in the celebration of love with us. We never did quite figure out where the music was coming from!

We were all guided and touched by this purely Angelic presence and my own internal experience was a profound recognition of this energy that I have felt before in times of need, and in times of grace and silence.

My second experience, which profoundly led me a significant shift internally, was the following year at the cottage. One night while sleeping in the bed next to my sister, I awoke to the strange sensation of falling into the bed. I felt as though my body was joining the boundaries of the bed, that I was the bed, and everything around me faded away. It was a deep vibration that seemed to reverberate into my body. This sensation continued for only a few minutes but it felt as though it was moving through my body and shifting the cells in my body.

I turned to my sister and shook her to awaken. She did not.

I felt no fear. In fact what I did feel was a strong sense of Angelic presence in the room. I felt such a peace that no words can describe; a longing, a belonging. I felt home. I began to pray and express gratitude for being here in my presence and knew that something larger than my own sense of my world was happening. And then I slept.

When I awoke in the morning, I asked my sister if she had felt anything "strange" last night. She said that she didn't.

That day I went down to the dock, lay my head down, and slept and rested for hours on the dock in the sun. I listened to the sound of the water gently whispering words of comfort and love to me. I listened to the familiar sound of the birds playing in the trees. I felt the sun on my face and I felt so blessed. My body was vibrating at a different speed. My crown was opening and reaching for the sun. I felt the presence of my own bigness and of the spiritual essence of the night before. I felt downloaded with a new sense of my awakened self.

At the time, I was nearing the end of a painful chapter of a dark night of the soul I had walked through. I was also at a crossroads in my heart about whether my long-felt path as an energy healer was going to work out for me: questions about whether I was in that category, questions about whether I was enough, and pondering my spiritual path silently within.

I am overwhelmed with the power of such a silent experience; humbled by the love I felt from deep inside my heart and soul. In the days following, I realized that what I felt, was me on a different level and depth that I had ever felt, touched by the subtle energies of something I couldn't see with my physical eyes.

The day I left the cottage, I went to sit and meditate at one of the local beaches just outside of the city. I felt profoundly different with a new sense of connectedness and passion for my journey. I knew it wouldn't be easy. Lessons are quite often not. But I was no stranger to obstacles. I felt supported by my Guides and Angels so intensely that while sitting on the beach, it was as though I was the only person in the world. I thought about my experience at the cottage and how peaceful I remembered feeling in that connection. My Angels reminded me that I could revisit that centre of silence at any time. And so, I do.

We are all humans. I am no more special than anyone else. Many feel that as ordinary people, they will only ever experience ordinary things. One thing I have learned through my life, through love and kindness, is that every experience, every word, every action and inaction is not ordinary. Everything has meaning. And the signs and symbols in the ordinary beauty of our lives are only waiting to be seen. If we open our eyes beyond the boundaries of what is just there, we can see people, situations, life very differently. Everything has meaning. Everything is a sign. These were two big ones for me out of many others I have experienced.

To this day, I call upon Michael when I am lost and in need of guidance and energetic protection. He is ever present in the energy work that I do and in my personal life. I understand with a deeper resonance that even when you feel so deeply alone in this world...you are never alone.

Angel Kiss

Angels of Love

Anu Shi Asta

Angels of Love bring you an important message about self-love. Many of you are suffering from loneliness, feelings of unworthiness, and the illusion of lack of love in your lives. The angels want to remind you that there is an abundance of love this Universe. The only reason why you may feel lack of love is because you are searching for it outside of yourself, but love is not something that can ever be separate from you. It is who you are, and to define love is to limit it. The Universe is created of love and you are made of love. One of the most rewarding, yet challenging exercises, is to tune into this limitless source of love within yourself. Open your heart to giving and receiving love through loving yourself first.

Self-love begins with allowing yourself to be happy and to live a fulfilling life. Make a conscious choice to let happiness into your life and bring down the walls that block your happiness. Learn to love yourself more by getting to know who you are more deeply. Begin asking yourself these questions: *"Who am I?", "What kind of a person or soul am I?" "What does my heart desire?"* The more you get to know yourself, your dreams, and your fears, the easier it becomes for you to accept yourself. When you meet a stranger, you won't immediately love them, but if you give them time to get to know who they are on the inside, your feelings for that person will grow. Spend time with yourself and allow yourself to fall in love with the beautiful dreams and desires you hold in your heart; even your insecurities become something you want to protect and heal when you are fully present with yourself. You will become more compassionate towards yourself and your life. You will soon discover a source of love within yourself.

Imagine feeling so much love for another person that it fills your heart. Perhaps you have felt this way about a lover, or your child. Do you think this love comes from this other person? Is the other person giving you this feeling? Actually, this love that fills your entire being is created within you, in you own heart chakra. Love is never outside of you, and when you realize that, you will have the power to experience love anywhere, anytime, and within yourself.

Call in the Angels of Love to help you open your heart and soul to the beauty and love that is inside of you. There are no limits to the miracles you will see unfold in your life with the power of love.

ANGEL KISS

INTUITION

Vanessa Krichbaum

I can't remember what age I was, but was old enough to understand the importance and depth of the words my grandmother spoke to me. We spent many hours in her sun-soaked kitchen, having wonderful talks while she cooked and I listened, watched, and learned. It was never just a cooking lesson, but lessons about her perspective on life. I only ever had two weeks each summer with my grandparents, as we lived in different provinces, but I cherished every second of every two-week visit.

I wish I could remember exactly what she was cooking on that particular day, but guaranteed, it was delicious and impressed me and my grandfather's taste buds! Nanny, as I called her, started to tell me a story about a time she was driving in a car with my grandfather. As they drove through the city, she started to have an overwhelming feeling of anxiety. As the anxiety grew, that not-so-little voice in her head told her she needed to get out of the car. The feeling grew stronger by the second and she told my grandfather about her fear and that they should stop the car. Of course, pragmatic man and exceptional driver that he was, this made no sense what-so-ever. They continued to drive and somewhere on route, another driver made a wrong turn and *whammo*...right into my grandparents' Volkswagen bus. Of course there were the pre-requisite dents in the vehicle, but everyone was fine.

My grandmother's moral of the story was to always trust that little (or big) voice in my head that tells me something. Whether it's a warning of an accident or to not trust someone, this is a voice to listen to. This was the first time anyone had spoken to me about intuition. It was not a well known topic or practice back in that day.

For many years I disregarded that voice. I learned lessons the hard way, proving my internal voice right and my practical self wrong. I spoke with many spiritual teachers who told me to trust myself and still, I persisted in not listening to me. The more I did not listen, the more out of alignment my life became and the more depressed I became, until, I just surrendered to not knowing what to do next.

That simple act of surrendering allowed the Angels to put in my path exactly the coaches and teachers I needed. I've learned valuable skills and practices that have helped me develop and most importantly, trust my intuition. My Intuition always supports my highest good and I increasingly see my life aligning to the beautiful vision I hold in my mind.

CHAPTER 4

THE GIFT OF LOVE

Brian D. Calhoun

People come and people go from our life, whether it is through death, an ending of a friendship or relationship, a change of location, change of employment, or for whatever other reasons and throughout it all, life continues on. With each of these endings you will process in your own way, and time. Some are easier than others to heal, process, and move through the grieving process. Some of us may get stuck along the way and not be able to find a way out of the grief that we are experiencing without some extra support.

When someone dies it can be challenging depending on the connection we had with the person on the earth. Often we process this is by connecting to the soul and talking with them along our journey about what is happening, how we miss them or by asking for help. This can be the first step for many to connecting with the Divine Love & Light of our Angelic Support Crew.

For others, the ending of a relationship can be an emotionally charged and trying period. We turn to our friends and family to help us process and deal with the conclusion of a relationship we may have thought or hoped was going to be for life. However, some people may feel that they can't turn to their loved ones to help them through it. Perhaps, it is due to the relationships that the family or friends formed with the ex or for other reasons. For these people, connecting to the Spiritual Realm may be the way to process their own personal feelings of grief with the loss of the relationship.

A change of venue within your career, home, or even city can also provoke feelings of grief for some. The changes that come with these experiences can sometimes be overwhelming or paralyzing in many ways for many people. Sure, we will meet new people as we settle into our new jobs, homes, or cities even as life will continue on. This temporary experience will eventually pass as we get grounded and centered in our new routines. However, we don't see these experiences of a form of mourning. At times we don't even make the connection that we are grieving the loss of what once was in our lives.

Death can even come in the form of some health crisis or challenge that is unfolding in life. Think about it, you are going about life and suddenly, you injure yourself and are laid up on crutches or worse, in bed for a period of recovery. You may have a serious health crisis such as heart issues, cancer, or something else. It can be something smaller such as a gallbladder rupture and discovering other minor issues at the same time. It may even be the loss of your healthy figure.

Whatever the issue, if it catches you off guard and causes you to make some changes to accommodate the experience, it can cause you to go into a bit of a tailspin as you make room for the new normal. Even if it's a temporary thing, you can be sure that you will be dealing with some aspect of this grieving process.

Each of these experiences are very natural and normal to each of us. I am sure you will agree having undergone many of these yourself. For myself growing up, I experienced many of these occurrences. As a child, I experienced death starting in my life when I was just a baby with the loss of my Aunt Dolly, and then shortly afterwards with the divorce of my parents. Death truly was a part of my life with lots of loved ones leaving the earth, each in their own time and way.

I also experienced grieving with school mates who left or transferred schools for personal reasons. Growing up, I also experienced people leaving my life to live their own, such as my father. Luckily for me, another father figure stepped up to the plate to assume the role at the time.

As an Intuitive & Empath, I felt more deeply than most and I didn't understand the reasons why I felt the way I did most times. So whenever people were grieving any life experiences that were unfolding, I absorbed their energy and took it on as my own. I believe I did this as a way of bringing some universal healing and peace to others.

I believe that as children we process grief in our own way. However, much of it we don't understand and thus forth never truly gets healed or released. I found myself turning inward much of the time and those around me truly never understood the pain I felt. Truth be told, I don't think I truly understood myself. Thankfully, I knew I wasn't alone and that there was something watching over me…my Angels and Guides.

Growing up we never really went to church on a consistent basis unless we happened to be with other family members, so I can't say that I called this invisible force Angels, or Guides, or even my Heavenly Loved Ones at first. That being said, I would often find myself talking with this invisible group of divine beings and well if I listened closely, I would often hear their voices. However, I did not share this with anyone else, as I already felt weird and left out much of the time. Many times it sounded like a softer more loving version of my own voice, so who was I to question if it wasn't my childhood fantasies at play?

As I got older and started on my path I found myself reaching out to Heaven and asking for assistance with everything from releasing me from a job that drained me, finding an apartment, or even helping me deal with issues that were bothering me at the time. As an adult dealing with the unexpected loss of my mom, I found myself eating my grief and pounds of pain and regaining the weight I had lost years before.

By this time I truly was tuned in and tapped in fully to the spiritual realm, so I once again asked for assistance, this time to help me get my eating under control and thus forth weight back done. My angels guided me to use a healing tool that they had gifted me during the early years of my path work, and well I found myself starting to heal and transform my body, mind, spirit, and emotions to match that of a Light and Trim person.

First, my Angels and I worked on the emotions and mental components of the reasons that I had gained weight, and why I was choosing the foods that I had been eating. Discovering much of it was connected to various levels of grief, other emotions and most of all the foods that my mom loved. This phase was very much like doing Therapy on myself; taking time to ponder and look deep within at the various points in life where I either gained or lost weight.

As I continued this therapeutic work, I was then guided to work with the healing and clearing statement that my guides gave me to clear the attachments to the foods that I found myself craving and addicted to. One by one, the shift began and I found myself starting to crave healthier foods. Once I got deep enough to the last keys, I turned off the Fat Switches and turned on the Thin Switches, setting the final steps into gear.

I began to lose the pounds of pain quickly, just like my Angels and Guides had told me that it would earlier in my journey. From the beginning of the physical weight loss to the end, it was just under one year. I don't think I was even prepared for how fast it melted off. And that was without exercise and with a very healthy eating routine now fully established. I found myself often searching for healthy versions of the foods I enjoyed so that I didn't feel like I was being deprived of my favorites to help with this transition.

The next steps on the healing journey was establishing a healthy exercise routine, followed by getting certified as a Personal Trainer. During my training and working with clients, I often found my connection to the Spiritual Realm helping people heal, transform, and love themselves fully. Their energy and guidance helped me to connect with my clients on a spiritual basis.

If you are needing some assistance, know that your Angelic Support Crew are awaiting your request, ready to serve you in every moment and way. For they see you as the CEO of the company, and won't do anything without your approval first. They love you so much that they will let you stay in your power and guide them in how they can best serve you until you ask for their help.

Angel Kiss

Street Angel

Tracy Lacroix

As I got to the bus terminal, I saw a man sitting on a bench with his hands over his head screaming repeatedly. There were many people in this area but not one person seemed to pay any attention to him. At first, I thought he may be mentally ill or coming off of drugs. The screaming got louder as the man began to walk around shouting at people, *"He was blue and no one cared!"* He repeated those words over and over. He approached several people but no one acknowledged him at all. I could feel the fear and sadness in his voice. This man was obviously very distraught. I felt so sorry for him but what could I do? He was heading my way, looking right at me. His ice blue eyes stared into mine. As he came closer, my heart began to beat faster. I wasn't sure what he was going to do. I heard a soft voice whisper, *"Do not fear him, bless him."* I felt complete empathy for him at this moment. He yelled right in my face, *"It could have been you!"* I looked straight into his eyes and said, *"Bless you!"* He yelled it even louder at me. Again, I said, *"Bless you."* It was not something I normally say. It almost felt as if time had stop at that moment. Everything got quiet. He was not yelling anymore and walked away. I felt a sense of calmness within me and with him, almost like we connected in some strange way. As I stood there wondering what just happened, I felt someone tap my shoulder. I turned around and the man had a big smile on his face and said, *"Thank you for listening."* I told him he was a very blessed man and asked why was he so upset. He told me he woke up that morning to find the man beside him dead on the street. He was traumatized and had no one to talk to since that was his only friend. I assure him that his friend was in a beautiful, peaceful place with the angels watching over him and didn't want him to be sad.

I felt people staring at me strangely but I didn't care. I knew this man needed to be heard, so I listened to what he had to say. I told him to share his smile with everyone, even if they didn't smile back.

As I thought about this man later that day, I realized he had a glow about him, his eyes, his energy, the connection I felt and no one noticed him. I realized then that I had just met an angel.

ANGEL KISS

SIGNS FROM BEYOND

Tracie Mahan

My story is about a kiss from Heaven. Years ago, when I was in High School, my brother's best friend was killed in a car accident. He was like a brother to me, as he was at our house quite often. It was a surreal moment when we got the news of his accident. They had him on life support for a couple days at the hospital, but there was no coming back from the injuries he endured. I remember being there with the family and my brother. How sobering it was to sit among them and feel their pain and grieving, yet holding hope for a miracle. "Shane" died shortly after, and that is when my real journey with him began.

The next experience I had with him was one I will never forget. I was at his funeral, not a dry eye in the room except mine. I could not figure out why I was feeling so light, happy, and free. I was about fourteen years old at the time and had no reference to communicating with a crossed love one at this level yet. I could feel the Angels around me and knew Shane was okay. It was the oddest feeling to know he was fine in the mists of all the tears filling the room. On the drive to the cemetery, I kept trying to cry, feeling like I was so insensitive to the family and to my brother, but I couldn't chase away the feeling of joy. That memory stuck with me for a very long time, as my journey into being a medium was not going to officially take off until a later date.

The accident that Shane had was on a route I later had to take every day to work. The tree they hit was still standing, with a cross as a memorial and a reminder. One day while driving past this tree I said out loud in my car, *"I love you Shane, and miss you."* That was the moment I felt, without a doubt, the kiss on my cheek. It was soon after that my life started to change, and synchronicity brought me to the life of a Medium and a Psychic. Shane continued to communicate with me for several years. I would receive daily signs from him and soon I was able to decipher his voice from mine in my head. I discovered we had other lifetimes together, and the connection to him was stronger than I thought. This is why I could sense him so strongly at the funeral that day. I felt his joy, and was given the gift of knowing he was in Heaven. Sometimes our Angels are our loved ones.

Open to the signs you are given, and know there is more waiting for you.

Chapter 5

Serenity

Deb Bergersen

Tears of joy well up in my eyes, as I begin to record my thoughts. So much synchronicity has happened in the last few days it is mind boggling. Our Angels and Guides align spiritual experiences and memories when we least expect it. Parts and pieces coming together in perfect timing. Our Guides and Angels orchestrating everything perfectly!

I just had a day where time was virtually stopped. All to allow us to show new/old friends why I love Sedona energy. We had a day when only six hours allowed for twelve hours of activities. How can it get better than this?

Where do I begin?

How does one put such deep feelings into mere words?

I have a passion for ancient relics. A passion for visiting sacred Native American sites, seeing the past come alive on the walls of the stones. I am blessed to have a partner who shares this passion. The two of us spend much of our time searching out history of the past.

As strange as it may sound to many, I feel such a connection to the land, to nature, the ancient trees and rocks, to the earth herself.

Spending time near red rocks makes me feel at home. They give me a feeling of safety and comfort. They seem to propel me into a different time and space. A time and space that I am reluctant to leave at times. Sometimes it feels as though characters are on a stage playing out the roles they had in that time. Whispering answers to the questions in my mind.

Have you ever been to a place that draws you in that way? To a place that you feel you know? Have you seen people you feel you have always known even when you first meet?

If you have you may understand a little more of what I feel in places with red rock. Sedona Arizona is one of those magical places for me even though it is not the only one.

Sedona is a very busy little town with hundreds of thousands of people who pass through it every year. The red of the rocks draws you into welcome you and the cedar trees give it a beautiful contrast. Many of the rock formations are named. There is Snoopy, the Sphinx, Lizard Rock, Thunder Mountain, Bell Rock, and Castle Rock to name a few. A little creek flows through the town which winds its way many miles to reach the Verde River. The Verde valley stands to the south east of it. This valley encompasses many small friendly towns which makes it a community much like it was thousands of years before when the Sinagua people lived there. The Sinagua lived in Pueblos, Cliff Dwellings and had many villages throughout the Verde Valley and along the Mogollon Rim. These show up approximately every mile. Very few remain as many have been decimated by pot hunters and people looking for artifacts. Walls have crumbled and fallen but this people left a rich history behind. Many Native tribes occupy this area and there remains a rich history from all of them.

What does any of this have to do with finding serenity? Really I am getting to that. I need to tell you a short story to explain and the short history above was to help you understand the nature of the land.

SACRED WALL

Mia had been to the sacred wall many times before but today was the first time she had been there with Tamar. This was someone who she had just met hours before yet felt like she had known for many, many years. Tamar had traveled a great distance to see this wall. Yet even she, had been to this wall before. Mia was also there with her husband Alan and Sadie, a friend of Tamar's. As we started down the path leading to the wall, Mia noted that Alan and Sadie were walking together a short distance ahead of Tamar and her. The space gave these two old friends a chance to discuss the visions the morning had brought for Tamar. It gave them the opportunity to remember. The two walked along the path chatting when suddenly Tamar stopped. *"Wait,"* she said, *"I can't move. I need to figure out why."* They stood silently for a moment as Tamar adjusted to the energy. Mia told Tamar what she had learned before about what they were about to see. This wall of petroglyphs was a very sacred place. The archeologists believe that is why it was never desecrated or robbed in the past. Both were then able to move towards the wall.

Thousands of years before, both Mia and Thea, had stood at this sacred spot to exchange information and celebrate the sun, celebrate a new planting season and celebrated the harvests. The clans represented by a Shaman from each clan. Each Shaman knowing how vital the sun was on their existence.

As the two reached the wall, Tamar stared with wide eyes at the sacred symbols on it. She listened intently to the docent tell the story of how the archaeologists saw the symbols. Mia looked again at the symbols and had a deep knowing that she had placed some of these ancient symbols here. She looked and found symbols she had never noticed before. Each, boldly standing out among the others .Mia pointed out Crane clan's symbol to Tamar. Whispering, she told her, *"I have been told that was my clan."* Tamar searched the wall for Eagle clan, smiling when she saw it. Mia could sense Tamar's relief and joy.

The wall told the story of when to plant each type of crop. It told when to harvest the crops. It told the story of birth and of death and rebirth. You see, this wall held a solar dial. Each equinox appeared at the proper passing of the sun. The clans were all there together, giving thanks and offerings of support for the other. These ancient people worked together, in harmony with Mother Earth. They were one with each other and nature.

As they finished appreciating the sacredness of the wall and its messages, the four who had entered started walking out along the path back to their car.

Mia commented, *"I wonder why they let that small dog in there?"* Everyone looked at her and asked, *"What dog?"* Mia was confused and said, *"The small white dog that couple had with them. It was on a leash but they don't allow pets in here. So I was surprised to see it here."* The group laughed and asked if she was in the same realm with the rest of them. Mia laughed with the group knowing something deeper had just transpired. Her mind going over each detail, wondering if she had been in another reality. She had clearly seen a small white dog with a couple at the wall. The dog was on a leash as they were walking away from the wall.

"Why did I see a dog?" Mia asked herself. *"Was this the same spirit dog who is around me?"*

Several days later this was answered by an unexpected voice. *"You had a contract from another time to have a meeting at that time and space."* The moment Mia heard this she knew this was a truth for her. So many questions came to Mia's mind. Each question leading to another. Each answer to another question.

When they reached the visitor's center bathroom breaks were taken before beginning the trip to the next site they were visiting that day. As each When they reached the visitor's center bathroom breaks were taken before beginning the trip to the next site they were visiting that day. As each

57

waited for their turn, Mia's eyes locked on a small portion of wooden fence with a blooming bush behind it. She pointed it out to Tamar and asked if she knew what type of blooms they were. Tamar didn't and neither did Mia, but "boxwood" came to mind.

This same scene came to Mia's mind days later on seeing a painting a friend of Tamar's had posted. It was so very similar and contained many images of guides and animal totems she had seen during their day together. Another sign? Mia thought so she immediately messaged Tamar to look at it and contacted the artist.

On Alan and Mia's drive back to their winter home that day another amazing thing happened that day. The car's radio suddenly switched stations. Neither of them had touched it so Mia paid attention to the song she was hearing. *"You Lead, I'll follow. Your hands hold my tomorrow."* Arriving at home she searched for the song knowing there was a message in the words. The song was "You Lead" sung by Jamie Grace. The message is still becoming clearer but she is confident the light will shine on it very soon.

For days after Tamar had returned home Mia searched through all the coincidences that had occurred. She searched for the answers, reflected on the beautiful connections that were made and dreamed of the future.

I don't know yet how Mia's story will end. You see the story is playing out, still finding links and connections. Each day a new step is reached. A new light is found. I have so much gratitude to my Guides and Angels for making it all happen.

SIGNS

Vanessa Krichbaum

My German grandmother, the same one who shared her knowledge of intuition, shared her love of nature with me. She was an avid gardener and all the little creatures frequented her glorious garden. Our favorite was the lady bug! Whoever found one first would let it rest and climb on our fingers and hands and gently take it to show the other. To this day I associate lady bugs with my grandmother and the sight of a lady bug is a sure indication they she is present around me. They show up in the most unexpected places at just the times when I need that extra support. Most recently, in the cold of winter, as I was wading through the death of a relationship, there in a room I been in many times before, was a ladybug. A reminder of my earth Angel grandmother. She was no longer alive but to me just the sight of her was a reminder of the eternal love that surrounds me.

However, the biggest sign of my grandmother's ongoing love and constancy came right after her death. I had been unsuccessfully shopping for a long brown suede coat for almost a year. When my grandmother died, the responsibility of clearing out her house fell to me and everything I was doing got put on hold. It was excruciating, going through her beloved home, where she had lived for the last forty-five years. All her precious things, antiques, paintings and china brought from Germany. Exquisite clothing fitting of the 5′ 10″ earth Angel beauty she was. Drawer by drawer and closet by closet I cleaned out her home. One of the last closets was the front hall closet. A real clothes horse, it was filled with coats for all seasons and occasions.

As I got to the last item at the back left of the closet, my hand could not believe what it felt; the most luxurious suede. And sure enough, out came the long, brown suede coat I had envisioned for so long. I made a point of wearing it right away as it made me feel wrapped in her love and protection. On a coffee run one afternoon, while I was still in the clean out process, the young lady at the coffee counter did a double take and said to me, *"Wasn't there just and old lady there with you?"* To which I replied, *"No, just me."* I smiled inside and felt full of warmth and love. My Nanny, now in the spirit world, was still right there with me.

I still have that gorgeous coat and I wear it every spring and fall. I walk tall and proud in it, the way she would have, knowing that her love surrounds me as she walks among the Angels now.

Chapter 6

Discovering my Life Purpose

Anu Shi Asta

"What is my Life Purpose?" One of the most beautiful questions a person can ask. When you find yourself raising that question, know that you are on a path of self-discovery and a magical transformation is about to begin. Souls all over the world are awakening to their purpose, ready to be ravished by fulfilled dreams. We all have unique gifts to contribute here on Earth and to create something wonderful together. Since I began asking that question, not only have I found a way to express my joy through work that I love, but I have unleashed my true essence as a divine creator making dreams come true. I have a vision of Heaven on Earth for us all and I believe it is possible. To me, it is a state of mind that can be reached by following inner guidance. I share my journey in hopes that it will inspire you to be all that you are meant to be.

I was born in Sweden and grew up in Finland in a typical non-religious Nordic household, raised by a single mom. My first memory of Angels was when I was about four or five years old. When I was afraid before going to sleep, I would ask the Angels to change the scary images in my mind to happier ones, and they always did. As a teenager, I had past life dreams about being in Ancient Egypt, which made me believe that soul survives death and that we are born again for a reason. As I was growing up, I felt the awakening desire to help others and make a difference. But I was feeling small, - *"There are so many people in the world in need, how could I ever make a difference?"* We all have an inner critic inside of us telling us how we aren't good enough, or smart enough to make a difference. Angels are wonderful in helping silence that inner critic.

I had my Angelic awakening when my first son Alex was born in 1995. I was just minutes away from giving birth to my baby boy when I noticed a woman in the delivery room wearing white hospital clothes. She was standing across the room and looking at me when everyone else was busy tending to me. When our eyes met, all of my pain was instantly gone in that very moment. It was as if she was brighter than anything in the room and she was smiling at me with compassion. In the midst of the intensity of childbirth, I suddenly found immense peace in her eyes. I turned away and when I looked back, she was gone. I knew in my heart, I'd seen an Angel.

Over the next few years while raising two sons, Angels would frequent my dreams; talking to me, clearing my energy, and even giving me healing messages. My inner world was getting richer but my marriage was falling apart. I had a vision of my very thin lifeline and I knew that I had to leave the unhealthy relationship. I believed that I needed to stay for my children's sake. However, my inner guidance made it clear that I should make a change for them and for me. So I left my material belongings behind and packed one suitcase filled with personal items and my children's things. Unfortunately, in the move I lost some childhood items and photographs.

Although we had nothing, we didn't truly lack anything. We moved to a small but cozy one bedroom fully furnished apartment and I found a job nearby. I never forgot my first night in that apartment: I made a cup of tea and squeezed the cup in my hands with so much gratitude. That cup of tea was a symbol of my new found freedom. There in front of me was a bookcase and I reached for a random book. It was a New Age psychological and spiritual book, which was the beginning of my transformation.

My past life dreams came back and as a result, I felt guided to see a past life regressionist. During my first session, I vividly remembered three lifetimes. As soon as I opened my eyes, I knew this was an important part of what I was meant to do in this current lifetime. I soon began my past life regression training and Angels were an essential part of my experience. They revealed a world of freedom, joy, and forgiveness. Soon after they also guided me to modify past life regression technique and they helped me to create a unique method entirely dedicated to working with Angels. Everyone who tried it was blown away by the power of this healing modality. I was often in tears of joy while witnessing miraculous things happening right before my eyes. I was now able to truly help people have powerful Angelic encounters and transform their lives, as the Angels were helping me transform mine. I had the most amazing healing technique I could have ever imagined but I was still an unknown healer. Deep within my soul I knew this method could transform the lives of thousands of people – and today it has.

I no longer wanted to work in an office, as it had already served its purpose in the past. That type of work did not feel meaningful to me anymore. *"How would I find clients to make my dream come true and was I even good enough to help others?"* I had no idea. My life was still a bit of a mess, but I asked Angels to help me do what I love and make it work. I couldn't continue at the office so I resigned with a couple of months to prepare my own spiritual business. It seemed quite foolish from a non-spiritual point of view; I had no other income, and I was a single mom of two young boys. But I had taken a leap of faith leaving my dysfunctional marriage behind. I knew I had to "jump" again and trust my inner guidance. I created a simple website and I had a mattress on my living room floor for my sessions. I had a client or two per week, not nearly enough to pay all my bills, but this is what I wanted and was guided to do.

Miraculously, Angels guided opportunities to me, even before I had fully left my office job. I was suddenly invited to do past life sessions and talk about Angels on Finnish national TV, radio, and magazines. I could hardly believe this was happening! I was an unknown Angel healer, but these opportunities were gifts from the Universe showing me support for living my purpose.

I was so grateful that I vowed to give back and in return, help the Angels. I gave my Angels permission to guide me towards the highest good of all. After saying this out loud, something strange happened. It reminded me of a movie where a spell is cast and magic moves throughout the body. I felt a powerful energy current move through me. For a moment, I was startled. I had now truly surrendered to my life purpose and in some ways my life was now in the hands of God, Universe, our Oneness.

My Angel business flourished and soon I published two books in Finnish. For a few years I travelled all around Finland every weekend teaching angel workshops and certifying healers for Angel Light Hypnosis. I was doing as many sessions as I wanted to do during the week. I was living my dream. Nothing stays the same and the soul constantly seeks ways to expand and grow.

In 2007 the Angels asked me to "jump" once again. I was guided to leave my successful Angel business in Finland and move to California with my two children to study psychology. It appeared on the surface to be a step back from my dream work, but in fact it was the opposite. I started thriving even more by finding out who I truly was and the same was happening with my children. I started over building a new business.

As I continued my studies at the University, I created online courses to continue working with my clients overseas and finding new ones in the US through my radio show and workshops. More of my soul purpose is being revealed to me every day as I am guided to do presentations all over the world. Angels have guided me to share the wisdom of Golden Atlantis to help souls remember what is possible for us all. The Angels shared with me that Atlanteans created a heaven on earth society where everyone thrived by doing what they loved. And I believe that a powerful step towards recreating that fulfillment in our modern world is for all of us to discover and fulfill our purposes as well.

May the Angels guide and support you along your life journey of discovery.

Angel kiss

Help is a song away
Brian D. Calhoun

Angels are always with us guiding, protecting, supporting, and blessing us with the love & wisdom of the light. People often think that some are more talented and connected to these divine beings, but in truth every soul has angels with them, whether they believe in them or not.

The angels are just an extension of divinity sent to be alongside with our soul journey to help remind us that we are not alone in the universe and that we are an important part of the universe. They help us to remember that we are the universe and that they are our helpers on the paths.

Often people are fearful to call upon Angels due to their own personal beliefs and upbringing in society. However, this is simply not true. Angels aren't associated with any one religion or way of living. They are the right arm of the Divine Source of Creation, Divinity, God, or any other name one may give the Great I AM.

Angels are with us when we are having good days, or bad, whether we are a place of grief, celebration, or going through some other journey in our lives. If we reach out to Heaven, they will gladly respond back to you. And everyone is capable of connecting with them and receiving their heavenly signs.

The angels love to have fun, for they say that when we are connecting to our inner child and just enjoying the moments with love and gratitude filling our hearts doing whatever makes us sing, laugh, dance, and play, we are at one of the closest vibrations to the source energy.

They say that one must remember to trust, have faith, let go, listen, and follow the guidance of the heart song at all times. When one does, miracles unfold greater than one may believe is possible. Nothing more than holding the belief that everything is possible when one believes in the power of LOVE to bless, heal, or transform our experiences and lives to sing in harmony alongside our heart song.

Angels can help keep our thoughts, actions, and choices based in love when we ask them to help do so, to help lift our energy and emotions up when we are down, or to improve the quality of our life experiences. It does not require any special skill or connection. All that is necessary is a willingness to believe that even before we consciously ask, the call has been answered, and the outcome is assured.

So when you are going through anything, or just want to fill your day with a sense of lightness, fun, and love, remember reach up to Heaven and know they are already blessing your day.

ANGEL KISS

NORTH TO ALASKA

Erica Johansen

I had fondly dreamt of visiting Alaska for years. I hadn't realized it would be for my Dad. Time had come to spread his ashes. The plan was to meet in Ketchikan with little knowledge how to get to Forrester Island, Dad's request.

The airplane landed. My thoughts drifted to the previous time there. As a child, Dad took me in his Cessna airplane. We flew over the snow-capped mountains of Alaska. I had complete faith and trust we would make it. At my age, I hadn't realized the dangers. Before flight, we prayed, asking angels to watch over us as we flew. Later in life, my father shared that we almost didn't make it. The clouds prevented him from seeing a mountainside that we were headed for with no sky in sight. All he could do was pray for a miracle. And it mystified him to that day how we lived!

My Dad was brilliant with an open-mind. He shared with our family tales of his previous lives and memories from other times and eras. He spoke of a life on Forrester Island as a boy fishing. In his recollections he had sadly drowned in an accident. Was it coincidence that in this life the disease that took him, started with fluid filling his lungs? His sincere wish was to be laid to rest at Forrester Island this lifetime after he passed.

I pulled my thoughts back in as we unloaded off the plane. I was to locate a curious fellow with a straight mustache. We made our introductions and with a, *"Let's go, let's go!"* I was shuttled into his fishing boat and across to the mainland to meet my brother. The gent strolled into the hotel and sat at my brother's table. *"So you're here to spread your Dad's ashes at Forrester Island. You'll need to get a plane. So come with me, I know where to take you."* It seemed unreal but away we went in his taxi boat in search of a plane.

We met a pilot who thought it best for flight today and to take-off shortly. Up in the air he shared he'd flown a handful of times to Forrester Island. Over the past hundred years the weather patterns had changed making it impossible to travel to the Island, let alone live or fish there. Only a handful of days in the year could one fly there and today we were lucky.

That day we laughed, cried, and celebrated a most amazing man! We spread Dad's ashes in the winds of Forrester Island. It was his way of taking his kids to Alaska one more time. On the flight back, the pilot suggested he land his float plane for a bathroom break. As children, there were no "bathroom breaks" flying with Dad. He'd joke, *"I need a float plane for when you kids need to go to the bathroom."* This was one last ride with Dad with a float plane!

We were blessed with synchronistic timing and the earthly and heavenly Angels who helped along the way. Time stood still! I'd say Angels orchestrated such a lovely day.

CHAPTER 7

THE ANGEL'S GIFT

Deb Bergersen

Have you ever noticed that our Angels have a way of making everything work out? In my last story, I told you about some amazing experiences with them slowing down time for my friends. The story continues a little at a time as each day passes.

Since my visit, I have returned to my home near Yellowstone Park and the Grand Teton National Park. It is not unusual there to see snow as late as July. The valley where I live is surrounded by mountains covered in pine trees and desert, yet this desert is different from Sedona. Parts of me are still vibrating on the energy of Sedona, whereas other parts are glad to be home.

Home is still much cooler than the glorious weather in Sedona in the spring. So my body is adjusting to cooler weather. Remnants of winter are still apparent here. The cooler weather means I don't get to explore as much as I would like to. I have also felt in limbo the last few days, but I keep hearing, *"You're not stuck, just to relax and let things play out as they are meant to be."* This advice comes from my Angels and guides (or "my team") which I feel is very sound. However, doing so can prove to be much more difficult.

During those days of feeling stuck, I had been attempting to work on a group project that was due in just a week. I would write a few words then my mind would wander away. Upon returning to the keyboard to write, I would begin something totally different. Normally when I write, the words seem to just flow. Not this time! I began questioning what I had to say about Angels. What did I have to share about them? My answers came:

"You have many things to share, you just have never thought of Us as Angels. You have to relax and let Us help." Later that day, a generous Earth Angel helped and more answers began to flow. The words below started spinning in my mind, each word eager to make its appearance known on the blank page.

The Gift

Mia's mind was racing through so many scenarios, she could barely keep up. The day had started so beautifully. She wasn't sure that anything could top it!

She woke after strange dreams about giant bugs! In the dream there were three large mantis and a giant bumblebee. She ran to get bug spray, and returned with ant spray that she couldn't use. She was mesmerized by the huge bumblebee. There was no way she could think of ending this beautiful creature's life. So she just watched them react to each other.

Mia got up and began doing her morning routine. She gave thanks for the earth, the day, all the wonderful messages she had received through the night, and the bright, beautiful sunshine, all the while reveling in the glorious sunrise. There were pinks, peach, purples, yellows, and gold all around her. It was such an uplifting sight to see. While connecting with nature she suddenly realized that she needed to look up the meaning of bumblebees in dreams.

Mia sat at her computer and started to research online for the meaning of giant bumblebees in dreams. She found several variations of meanings. Two sites had exactly the same words: *"If bumblebee finds you, you must follow its lead. If you do this you will come to the destination most suited for your new life awakening."*

That's it, she thought. The words of the song "You Lead", by Jamie Grace, came rushing back to her. That is why my team gave me that song!

She then started her chores. Laundry started, she sat at the computer and started to type. Looking up, she noticed she had a message from her team leader on the new project. As she clicked over to read the message, her heart began to radiate. She was feeling the love of her guides and Angels. It surrounded her being making her feel empowered.

The message was exactly what she had wished for just the night before. She was given the opportunity to tell more of her journey. Mia could barely contain her joy! When she first became involved in the project, she only had one small part to play. However, her part continued to expand. This new opportunity had made her dreams of sharing her passions become a bigger part of her reality. She remembered the time she had first dreamed of sharing her passion. Mia realized the dream had been with her since she was a young child in school. She had changed the direction she was headed in, as she explored another path.

Alan, her husband, wanted her to go with him to a nearby town as he ran an errand. Thoughts of the project ran through her mind as they drove the thirty miles to the nearby town. As they drove, she noticed how gray the day had become. Rain clouds had moved in. It was raining heavily now as they traveled along the freeway. Suddenly Alan swerved the car. Mia looked up startled from her thoughts. A semi-truck was coming into the lane they were in as they were passing it. Shocked and a little shaken, Mia noticed the driver was cursing at them. Mia shook her head and laughed, sending love out to the driver as she did. Then she took note of the sky in the distance. It was bright and sunny, the mountains with their snow caps gleaming in the sunlight. Right over them was darker, as tends to happen during the rain, yet it was sunny in the distance. It was her Angels and Guides giving her a sign that things would work out right.

By the time they arrived at their destination, the rain had stopped. Everything smelled clean and fresh. The rain appeared to have washed all her troubled thoughts away. She smiled and went about the next few hours just enjoying each moment. Each breath bringing new energy and clarity to her soul.

The return trip home was pure joy. Each tree shouting their beauty out to Mia. The lava beds were shining and the cedar trees growing stubbornly out of the lava, showing their strength. She could hardly contain excitement to begin the expansion of her part of the project. Other little signs were still appearing. She noticed the date 4/4. She noticed times she had sent messages 9:44:44, 5:44, 10:44. *"Angels!"* she thought. Laughing, she silently thanked her team for their support. Mia knew just how much they helped in making this gift happen for her.

Mia remembered a thought from just a few days before; about many messages she had seen over the last few months all urging her to step out of her comfort zone and become more open with her feelings. Mia had taken steps in that direction which brought up fears but she kept moving forward one step at a time.

She remembered the stranger's words to her years ago asking, *"Are you still writing?"* Mia remembered looking at the stranger in confusion and saying, *"I don't write."* Months later, another person asked the same question. The scenario continued to happen until she finally started researching what it would take to publish a book. Her research had taught her that saving some additional funds out of her small income would be necessary.

In the meantime, she journaled. Writing something in her journal daily for over two years, it became part of her daily routine. Her friend Krystal challenged her to write, so Mia began by writing and sharing a blog. For a while she published something each day, then one day the words stopped flowing. No matter what she put to paper it didn't feel right. So the blog became more of an occasional task. As a very private person, Mia felt so revealed and exposed to the public. Had fear gotten in the way? Had the ego yelled at her? She did wonder. Mia continued to trust that if her dream were to come true, her Angels would help her somehow.

Mia remembered thinking the door would open and the right opportunity would appear. Had that door opened? Had the simple acceptance of an opportunity to participate in this project opened that door? Mia was so grateful to her friend for the invitation to join the project. She realized she not only had her Heavenly team to be grateful for, but also several Earth Angels as well. Mia's gratitude for the opportunity poured from her heart to those special Angels who have helped so much on this part of her journey.

As Mia's story found its way to paper, I was reminded of many other times when my Heavenly Team have given me direction and held my hand throughout my fears. To all my special Earth Angels, I send my love and deep gratitude. Thank you for being in my life! Blessings surround us all. We only have to remember to receive them. Angels, Ancestors, and other Guides are always there for us. We just need to ask and take a step along the path we have chosen.

I don't know where the next step of the journey will take me, but I am open to explore the adventures it provides me.

Angel Kiss

Three Boys

Tracie Mahan

There are many times Angels will come to us through our dreams and give us messages. We will see them as loved ones, family members, or familiar people who communicate with us. These dreams may even be prophetic. I had such a dream just months after my first son was born. The details of this dream were so clear and vivid.

In the dream, I was in my grandparents' house when I noticed a familiar and famous psychic there with me. We moved over to the couch in the family room and sat down together. She looked at me and asked me if I had any questions for her. I asked her how many kids I was going to have. She told me I already knew the answer to that question (which was true because I did a meditation earlier that week and got the answer!). Then she went on to tell me I would have three boys, and that one boy would be harder than the other two. I worried about why one of the boys was going to be harder than the other two, but in the years to come I would find out why.

A few years later, I was pregnant with my second child, and sure enough it was another boy. This was exciting to me because the dream was actually coming true. Soon after my second son was born, I had another dream. This time I heard a baby crying. I checked in the crib and lying there was a brand new baby. I picked him up and I could not break eye contact with him. I was instantly in love with this baby, and I knew if I looked away for even a moment, I would wake up and the dream would be over. It was so powerful, so real, so mesmerizing. In the dream, my oldest son asked to hold the baby and when I handed him over, I woke up. I knew intuitively that the baby in the dream would be my third son.

About a year later I was told by spirit that I would become pregnant with another son in February, and indeed I did. The dream had come true. Three boys! The third boy was the most challenging as I faced a divorce shortly after his birth. Then started my journey as a single mom, raising three great boys. The Angels knew I had quite a journey ahead of me and they were letting me know it was all divine and perfect. It helped me to trust my path and to know I was going to be supported by these angelic beings.

Compiled by Jewels Rafter

ANGEL KISS

THE LIGHT AND LOVE OF CHILDREN
Maureen Sullivan

I have worked in the Social Work world as a counselor for almost twenty years. I work in a program that supports women and children with trauma related to witnessing or experiencing domestic violence. My life is filled with the energy of children in my job, but I am also surrounded by my friend's little ones and my God children. Children are pure vessels of love and their wisdom runs deeper than our world sometimes allows for. They see all worlds from a different lens; one of clarity, belief, and magic! Perhaps it is another aspect of myself that is able to see, but I have been blessed with being witness to so many beautiful and enriching Angelic kisses in my world of children.

From a child talking intensely to a statue of Mother Mary and bringing me a message of hope, to a child sitting in my office and asking if it was permissible to have their Angel friend present who whispers words of encouragement to them, I have had several of those! Welcome all, I say. I have met a child who shares that she sees and feels wings around others, and child who talks about deceased loved ones as Angels not because they have been told by their adult world, but because they have a knowing and belief. One child, while on my healing table, asked about why the energy around them felt like the soft brushing of Angel wings on their skin. I call these Angel kisses.

I have a picture of a beautiful Angel on my bulletin board, surrounded by pictures from the Fae world. It seems as though it is a calling card children recognize. I have the same in my private healing room where I have treated children many times.

There are children who you meet that naturally gravitate towards you. There is this invisible force of recognition and love that locks your eyes. It's almost as if they are asking if you see them or know them too. They are emerging Earth Angels. Children recognize light and they see your light; our light. They want you to recognize this energy and to ask them about it. They are looking for that in you! I have learned so much in my lifetime, most of it from the wisdom and insights of children. They are our Earth Angels as they will be our greatest teachers of love and compassion. I honor them, their innocence, and their ability to just be in their present in their experiences! They teach us that Angelic beings and Spirits are around us always, lovingly guiding us.

So when a child says to me that their bedtime Angel comes to say goodnight, I truly believe them as I had a bedtime Angel too!

Compiled by Jewels Rafter

SECTION 2
Divine Communication

SECTION 2

DIVINE COMMUNICATION

Jewels Rafter

Communicating with your Angelic and Spirit Guides is not as complicated as one may think! In essence, all that is required is an open spirit and an awareness of your inner voice.

Our Guides and Angels are in constant communication with us, although we must be in listening mode in order to hear them and decipher their messages. One way calibrate that process is to have regular communication sessions in which you dedicate time to be still, listen for their guidance, and talk to them about what is occurring in your life. This helps you become accustomed to the type of connection you have with your Angelic Guides and this gets you in the habit of listening for messages. Our guides have specific and individual ways of talking to you, so how you choose to communicate with your Guide may differ from another person's method.

Some may use automatic writing, or ask for messages in their dreams or even through meditation. Automatic writing is a fabulous way of channeling your Angels or Spirit Guides through writing. It is a way to channel information and spirit energy through writing. It is the ability to allow intuition from outside you to flow through you. Automatic writing is a form of intuition that has been around for thousands of years. It allows you to "download" spirit's perspective subconsciously and transcribe it as it comes in. The key is to clear your mind, ask a question, and let the answer flow. Then without thinking too hard, simply type or write down the answers that come through. Automatic writing works, regardless of whether you write on paper or type from a computer keyboard. Find a calm and quiet place. Pay attention to your breathing. You may even want to visualize a bridge between you and the source you are seeking. Some people imagine an open window or door. What's essential is that you relax and clear your energy. Once you are in a positive and calm frame of mind, let the messages flow.

These messages come from an amalgamation of sources that include our higher self, our Angels and Guides, and other celestial energies who can offer support and guidance. During our lifetime on earth we may change Guides many times as we progress through our healing and awakening journey. When you set an intention for only the highest possible energies to be present when you speak to your Angels and Guides, you can be assured that you will not be contacted by any lower vibrating energies. That said, fear is a powerful attractor so be aware that when you ask for help out of fear or desperation, this places you at a lower energetic level and that can impact the types of the energies who try to connect with you. It's always a good idea to breathe and ground yourself energetically, connecting with heaven and earth, when you communicate with your Guides and Angels. Ask that only the most wholesome, loving beings, who live in the Light, be the ones who connect with you.

While the messages from these Divine Beings derive from the highest energetic frequency, it is filtered through our own energy, including our own fears. We cannot receive information that vibrates at a higher level than our own. Therefore this is why it is crucial to release any fears about communicating with your Guides, as lower vibrating emotions create feelings of confusion and uncertainty.

Our spiritual team guides us but they can't tell us exactly what to do. Consequently, when we ask questions from a place of uncertainty, we limit how they can respond. *"Show me the lesson I am intended to learn in this situation and how can I move forward,"* is more likely to receive a response than, *"Tell me what to do."* Remember that they don't necessarily know what is best for us. However, they are aware of what the potential next steps may be. You see, it is our own frame of thought and how we respond to situations that determines what happens next on our journey.

Asking for validations or requesting clear signs will not offend them. As far as trusting the information, you won't insult your spiritual team by asking them for confirmation. Asking for validation can entail a request such as, *"Please send me confirmation of this message, in the highest and best possible way within the next 24 hours so that it is absolutely clear to me."* Then make sure your antennae's are up and that you are in listening and receiving mode so that you receive the messages.

Your guides are aware of many different possibilities but you can only connect with those that are at your energetic vibration. They can't show you all of the possibilities unless you are open to those options. This is why it is important to be aware of your fears and to be open to many alternative options. The more you are willing to be open to your highest potential, the more you will be aware of new ways of being. That is what they can communicate with you but only when you are open and willing to listen. Angels will never tell you anything "negative" or mislead you, but you should always trust your own judgment and intuition. If an answer doesn't "feel" right, ask what source it is coming from, or request a concise confirmation and then make your choice based on what feels accurate to you. Messages from your Angelic Guides should always come from a place of unconditional love and consist of uplifting, supportive messages.

Prior to partaking in any clairvoyant or mediumship readings with clients, I always call upon my Angelic and Spirit Guides to come through and help to provide messages that are only my clients' highest good. Before communicating with your own team of Angels, ask them to surround you in white light and bring only messages from a place of unconditional love and healing. This will ensure that you will receive messages from only high vibrating untainted sources.

Doing what I do for a living, I am blessed with the ability to connect with passed loved ones. So I wanted to share another beautiful experience I had with one of my lovely clients.

This dear soul came to me in search of some light at the end of the tunnel. As she walked into my office this beautiful thirty-year-old woman looked as though the life had been sucked right out of her. Her energy was so low and her face looked like she had not had any sleep in months. I just wanted to surround her with so much love that my heart ached. She sat down and instantly I felt a young boy by her side. The child looked like he was perhaps four or five years of age. We started the reading and she asked a few questions about her career and financial status. However I felt this was not the reason she was here. I felt a huge void around her and a sense of immense loss. I could sense that she was in search of a sign or a message from the other side that there is more to life than this heartache. The child's energy was still very strong around her so I asked my Angels to ask him why he was here. All I heard was that there were tiny bubbles in the sky.

Knowing that most messages that come through from spirit make no sense to me personally, I asked her if she understood what that message meant. She looked at me with wide eyes and burst into tears. She explained that a year ago she had lost her four-year-old son and her husband in a car accident. However prior to this huge loss, her father also passed away and she had to explain the concept of death to her child. She explained to her son that a person's spirit goes up to heaven like tiny bubbles do, when they float up to the sky. When they reach the sky, an Angel is present to meet them with open arms.

Her son was confirming that yes, his spirit indeed floated up to heaven like tiny bubbles in the sky. We both sat there in tears feeling the love coming from this beautiful spirit. At that very moment she felt closure and her healing began.

Although we may question whether life exists after death, I have seen time and time again that our spirit lives on. We simply move to another dimension and watch over our loved ones on the earth plane. If you have lost someone dear, please know that they are not lost to us. But rather, they have moved on to a beautiful place and dimension where suffering and pain no longer exists. Talk to them, send them your love, and quiet your mind. I promise that you will feel their presence surrounding you when you least expect it. Time heals the pain but not always the physical void. However, there will always be a bond that holds them close to us.

When we have questions or need to feel support from the Heavens, call upon your Angels, Guides, or loved ones for a message. One way or another, you will sense their presence.

CHAPTER 8

MANIFESTING WITH THE ARCHANGELS

Anu Shi Asta

You have a rich inner life with beautiful dreams that live inside of your heart. Those dreams are signs from your soul, like a roadmap to follow your light path, and they are meant to be fulfilled. Angels wish you to live a truly happy life as you are meant to live, but there is also a higher purpose for having beautiful dreams pouring into your mind from your heart and soul. Happy dreams carry the energy of light, love, and joy so when you allow these dreams to materialize, you are making this world a better place as the world will be filled with more light. Your Angels will do anything in their power to help you and they ask that you spend quiet time sitting with your soul and listening to the dreams within you. As you become clear of what your heart truly desires, then call on your Angels to help you have faith in your dreams and to guide you.

The Archangels are mighty beings of light that oversee other Angels. They are a wonderful support for manifesting your dreams. There is an enormous amount of Archangels in the Universe. From the beginning of Earth time, we have had fifteen main Archangels on our Earth. Most renowned are Michael, Raphael, Uriel, and Gabriel as they are also mentioned in the Bible. But Angels are not attached to any human religion or race. They are here for all of us and are dedicated to help us create a better world for us all, starting with you. Angels and Archangels do not have a gender, because they are simply pure light. The Archangels are often pictured male, but some of the Archangels are commonly depicted female.

Let me introduce you to a few Archangels that would love to guide you and get you started, right away.

Archangel Michael

Michael is the Archangel of the Blue ray or protection and courage. First of all, Michael will help you get clarity to what exactly it is that your soul dreams about and shows you the steps needed to make them happen. Ask Michael also to cut away all attachments to dreams that are not your own. We often carry dreams that we have taken in from our parents, friends, the media, and through our society. Make sure the dreams are yours truly.

Michael is a powerful warrior Angel that will help you channel your inner warrior of light to fight for your dreams even if you are afraid or doubtful. When you work with Michael, you may notice an increase in determination and inner strength. Don't let anything get in the way of manifesting dreams that will serve yours and everyone else's Highest Good. You are a warrior of Light. You can do it!

Archangel Ariel

Ariel is the Archangel that is overseeing nature. Mother Earth provides us all that we need not only to survive on this planet but to prosper. We are living in a true Garden of Eden with abundance everywhere. As humans have lost their connection with nature, we have also placed ourselves in the energy of lack. Ariel can help you create a prosperous life not only by helping you manifest all the money you need to live but an abundance of grateful moments and magical experiences. Ariel will help you get into the flow of prosperity. She can help you find a new job, start a business, manifest new home appliances, help you find a way to finance your new home, etc. As you see your everyday material needs provided, there will be truly no limits to the abundance you can experience.

Archangel Gabriel

Are you looking for your life purpose? All the Angels can help you become more aware of your soul's agenda here on Earth but Archangel Gabriel of white ray brings you the message of your soul from the Source and guides you with each step you take. Gabriel is wonderful Angel to have around for those who wish to write a book or to create an online course for example. He will help you deliver your message to this world.

Archangel Zadkiel

Archangel Zadkiel the Angels of the violet ray of magic and transmutation. He is a magnificent Angel to help you work the magic and bring your dreams into reality. He can help you get in touch with the Midas touch within you and make the impossible, possible. He can help you transmute heavier energies into love and light so that any blocks in your body or life will no longer hinder your manifestation.

Zadkiel will help you awaken the magic touch within to change lack into prosperity, sadness to joy and fear into love. You can meditate and imagine

Violet golden silver flame burning away all lower energies from your life. Violet flame is a very powerful tool to cleanse away the old and make room for new.

Archangel Raziel

Raziel is a truly amazing Angel of Divine Magic. He has the knowledge of the mysteries of the Universe so he is a wonderful Archangel to have close by for those souls that are open and willing to break free from the illusions of our world. One realization after another he will help you uncover the magic of manifesting and help you master it. His intention is to help you remember who you truly are, that you are bright being of Light with the creative powers of God. He will help you manifest your dreams into reality and stretch your imagination to what you believe is possible. He may ask you questions like, *"Do you believe that you can fly?"* and to encourage you to dream bigger and higher. Anything is possible with his help.

Archangel Raphael

Raphael is the Archangel of the emerald green ray of healing and abundance. We often call upon him and his Angels to help our body heal. Indeed, he is a powerful healing Angel, a Chief medical officer, and Master surgeon in heavens. However, Raphael's healing powers and expert abilities extend far beyond medicine. If you wish to be a lightworker or a healer, he will teach you how to become one and also he will bring clients to you that will benefit from your unique gift. Many lightworkers feel guilty about receiving money for spiritual work and Raphael will help to remove those blocks so that they can better serve humanity while being in the balance of giving and receiving. If you are dreaming about a spiritual business or healing your finances, ask Raphael to help you heal away any beliefs that no longer serve you. The world needs more healers and you can ask Raphael to give you ideas on how you can make a difference.

Archangel Jophiel

Jophiel is the Archangel of beauty and clarity. She can help you clear out any confusion about what your dreams truly are and fill them with light. She is also helps you light your vibration to attract more beauty. Imagine a garden of love in your heart, a place within you where your dreams live.

In this garden you may imagine Angels, unicorns, rainbows, waterfalls, flowers of heavenly colors. Also when you go to this garden within your heart, you can meet your twin soul or your soulmate, or to feel what it's like to have a beautiful home and a beautiful life. Now that you experience so much beauty within yourself, it will begin unfolding in your physical life as well. Jophiel helps you become fully aligned with your beautiful dreams and to attract all that you need to fulfill them. Not only does Jophiel help tune into the beauty within your heart, but he also helps you see the beauty in your life, in other people, and in your past life experiences. Gratitude is the most powerful force you can add to your manifesting practice. Ask Jophiel to help you find more and more reasons to be grateful for. It is possible to create a heaven on earth because Heaven on Earth truly is a state of mind.

Archangel Chamuel

Chamuel is the Archangel of love and peaceful relationships. He carries beautiful pink energy that will heal your heart of the hurt and disappointment from your past relationships and will help you restore your faith in true love, the unconditional love. If you are looking to manifest your soulmate or even feel ready for your twin flame, then Chamuel can help you bring your souls together and guide you to a fresh start. If your current relationship needs healing or a peaceful ending, she can help you with that as well. Ask Chamuel and the Angels of love to be present whenever you are communicating with your significant other about difficult relationship matters or ask them to accompany you to your first date so that it will be a very romantic experience for both of you.

Call upon the Archangels whenever you need some guidance and they will bring so much happiness and joy to your life!

ANGEL KISS

MESSAGES OF LOVE
Brian D. Calhoun

Divine Communications come in a variety of ways, and you just never know when you are going to receive one. You will know that the message is true when the message received resonates and is pertinent to something unfolding in your experiences. It will be filled with a feeling of love, hope, and uplift you with healing and enlightenment. And if you are open to it, it will help you connect deeper to the power, wisdom, and energy of your soul.

The messages will be granted over and over to you until you truly recognize the communication and take appropriate action. It may be subtle like a whisper, or it may come in a stronger way, as the Angelic Messengers know exactly how to get you to stand up and pay attention. If that requires multiple transmissions of the same message through a variety of sources, so be it.

Today, such a message is offered to you as we know that some of you have been going through a dark night of the soul and have felt abandoned in some manner in your life, like no one upstairs is listening to or cares about your cries for help. This cannot be further from the truth. We hear every thought, word, and emotion you share in every way possible and always answer the call.

Many times what happens though is that you are hoping for a particular outcome. We are working to bring you through the experience better than you can ever ask for. We ask that you relax and know that we are working on the divine solution to everything that has caused you fear, worry, or concern. Along with working to bring forth more joy into your life through the fulfillment of you hopes, wishes, and dreams, we are listening to your cries deep within the heart while checking with your divine soul plan. We then combine all the wisdom of the universe to assist you with everything.

Like an onion, there is always multiple layers to every request and we listen to all aspects. We know that you are focused on one or two of the situations weighing your heart down and we take those serious as well. However, you as a soul being came into this world with the intention that we would steer you along the right pathways in the most gentlest of ways. You trusted us to know what was best for all concerned and work it out in some divine ways, knowing that we could see the bigger picture and guide you so.

Today, we ask you to surrender trust and have faith for we are on the case and everything is going to work out for the highest good. For you are never alone, EVER!

Much Love,

Your Angels

Chapter 9

Calling on the Angels

Tracy Lacroix

I knew I was in a bad situation with no way of getting out of it. It was late at night in a dangerous neighborhood. The buses were no longer running, the energy in the room started to feel heavy, and the person I was with was acting different, making me nervous. I knew something was about to happen to me. I should've listened to the signs I had gotten and my inner voice telling me earlier not to meet up with him. What else could I do but to close my eyes, take a deep breath, and call on the Angels to protect me. As I said each name (Archangel Michael, Raphael, Gabriel, etc.,) I could feel a strong, protective presence inside and surrounding my body. It felt like a shield of light was all around me. I continued to focus on this wonderful sensation. I remember feeling this before traumatic events in my life but never this strong or as loving. I heard a gentle voice tell me, *"Everything will be okay. You will get through this."*

"Do not open your eyes." I was curious to see who was speaking. I had heard this voice earlier that day but couldn't figure out who it was. As I opened my eyes, instantly I knew my life was in danger. The guy I thought was a friend was standing over me with a blank look in his eyes and the room was filled with men. Everything went dark, except for the two large beautiful Angels above me in a golden white light. I was feeling less afraid as my body became lighter, surrounded by the golden white light. Next thing I knew, I was looking down on myself and the situation. It was horrifying! I wanted to fight for my life but felt helpless as I was no longer in my body.

I heard the Angels say, *"Come with me."* I followed them through a large tunnel of light to a beautiful room. I was shown many different stages of my life that I had blocked from my memory, beginning as a young child. As each event was shown to me, I was reliving the sadness, pain, and fear that went along with it. I tried to look away but the Angels told me it was important that I remember all that I had been through in my life. *"These times where you felt alone and scared, we were with you."* I could feel the presence of many of my loved ones around me. I couldn't see who they were exactly, just a sense of how I remembered them when they were alive. I was then shown recent moments of me dealing with alcohol, depression, and abusive relationships. I was confused on why I needed to see this. I was two months sober, I was no longer depressed, and had chosen to be celibate. I had changed my lifestyle completely.

I was beginning to think I was not going to make it through this night. I couldn't see a way out of this situation. I didn't want my life to end, especially not like this! I wanted to return to my body to fight for my life. There was so much more I wanted to do with my life. My will to live became very strong! I was unsure of how I would get out of this situation or even move past what these people were doing to me without relapsing in my sobriety. I sat there reflecting on my life, feeling so hopeless. I didn't know if I could possibly go through it all again or if I even wanted to. I was tired of being a survivor of life! I was finally at a point where I had overcome it all. So how did I get myself in this situation? Why was all this happening to me?

I was guided to a beautiful, peaceful place with open fields, bright vibrant colors, and the most amazing waterfall. It felt so familiar to me, as if I had been in this place before. I found myself sitting under a large tree looking at all the beauty around me. I felt someone sit beside me and say, *"You don't have to go back if you don't want to. You have a choice."* A sense of relief came over me. At this point I was okay with dying. If this is how my life was supposed to end, so be it! First he wanted to show me what my life would be like if I did choose to go back. I was expecting to see myself in the hospital trying to recover mentally, physically, or worse but instead I was sober, happy, doing all the things I worked so hard towards and dreamt of all my life. I couldn't understand how that was even possible. He told me it was not my time. *"You needed to go through this in order for you to help others. There would be big changes in your life. Some things may be difficult but needed to change in order for me to have this life."* He told me when I came back, I would have many gifts available to me. He asked if I wanted them all at once or if I wanted to work for them. I said, *"When have I ever taken the easy road? I will work for them."* He told me that was a good answer. *"You will only know what you need to know about this night."*

Next thing I knew, I was back in my body, very confused, no memory of the night, the assault or the Angels. The energy in the house was calm, yet I felt like I needed to run. I heard a gentle voice telling me I needed to get out of there *now!* As I walked quickly down the street in this unfamiliar shady neighborhood, I felt very protected as if nothing or no one could harm me. When I got home, I slept deeply until the next evening. I woke up feeling like something was different about me. I looked the same but my soul felt lighter. I knew something had happened to me but didn't know what.

I felt the presence of the Angels almost daily and would hear messages as I would wake every morning. It was about a week before the memories of that night came flooding back. Of course it was only bits and pieces of what I needed to know. With each memory I would hear a gentle voice comforting me, assuring me I was safe from harm. These visions I was seeing had already happened. It could not harm me in anyway, unless I allowed it to. I began to meditate for hours every day trying to remember more of what happened. Each time I would become more spiritual, more connected to the Angels. I knew what I had been through was a huge lesson for me, a second chance at life.

I began reading books about Angels, healing, spirituality, energies, and pretty much anything that was presented to me. I was seeking a way to heal myself so I wouldn't become depressed or lose my mind. I couldn't talk to anyone about my experience as it sounded crazy. I started writing about it and seeking out spiritual advisors to help with answers. It seemed everyone I came across was familiar to me, as if I knew I was going to meet them, or they were expecting me. I would have enlightening conversations and sometimes it would trigger a memory with a message to follow. I would walk away feeling confident that I had just spoke to an Angel.

My awareness of people's energies began to heighten along with my intuition. I wasn't going to allow anything to stand in the way of my happiness or my sobriety! I knew that I was protected by my Angels and was given a second chance at life. I am grateful for everything I had gone through and value each lesson along the way. I am still unsure of what happened to me that night. I realized that it's not important. The past is in the past. It was the lessons I learned along the way that I needed to focus on. I made many changes in my life, attending workshops, classes, and learning. I became an advance Reiki and Integrated Energy Therapy Practitioner working with the Angels to help others move forward in life. My love and compassion for helping others through difficult times has helped me grow as well. My life has never been so fulfilling!

My dream of being happy finally came true, as promised by the Angels. The presence of my Angels, although I may not feel them all the time, has help me believe that no matter what you are going through, you are never alone. Call on the Angels. They are always listening.

Compiled by Jewels Rafter

ANGEL KISS

ANGELS WORK IN MYSTERIOUS WAYS

Julie Dudley

You've probably already noticed at some point in your life, Angels trying to communicate with you; through number patterns, scents in the air, or your dreams. Some would expect these loving beings to be present in happy times, and other times in hardships.

My experience involves both:

I was excited to find out I was pregnant with a second son, but I had a series of stressful incidents including domestic abuse and robbery. As a result, my doctor put me on bed rest. I really had no idea what would happen, so my son and I went to stay at my parents' house. Little did I know that the Angels would step in! It was as though Angel signs were everywhere. My doctor even had a collection of angel statues in her office. It was not a coincidence that my room at my parents' house had an angel painting on the wall and I found two white feathers within the first week of my stay there. It seemed that every time I looked at a clock it had either a series of number threes or number ones.

One night when everyone was asleep, I felt overwhelmed and sad. I couldn't stop crying, so I went into the washroom and turned the water on so nobody would hear me cry. Suddenly I felt warmth as though I was being hugged and comforted. I started to sing softly to the baby, and felt a sense of peace. Anytime I'd worry too much or feel sad, I would instantly feel a warmth around me and positive thoughts would come to mind. Time flew by and between my mom's optimism and the Angels who were by my side, I felt unconditional love. Angels will do this if you allow them to.

Before I knew it, the nurse came for her last house visit and told me it was okay to resume normal activity. That night I sat in bed feeling grateful for my mother's, father's, and the Angels' help. While in this state of gratitude, the warmth came over me again and I fell asleep with pleasant dreams.

The day he was born, I received the best birthday gift a woman could ask for; a beautiful son. Tears of joy came pouring out, warmth filled the room, and everything was blissful. It was only fitting to choose an angelic name, so I chose Gabriel. To this day, Gabriel has been a reminder for me to appreciate life and that the Angels are always there for you.

If you tune into the Angels, you'll be in for an amazing journey filled with love, comfort, and your blessings will be countless.

Chapter 10

Between both worlds

Tracie Mahan

All of my adult life I have spoken to the Angels, to the crossed over loved ones, and even to the ones I refer to as my council. The magic that I experienced in my life, when I opened up to this reality of the benevolent beings, is one I would never want to give up or loose. It brought me to a place in my own world that I didn't know was possible. To me, there is no going back. Once I experienced God and my Angels to this level, my life was changed forever.

At first my journey to connect with the Angels and loved ones was slow. I had to maneuver around old belief systems and old programming that limited my ability to communicate with intention. So many stigmas went with telling one's future, or speaking to loved ones who have crossed over. So many false fears wrapped around the idea of talking to "The Dead." I had always been taught that God did not want us to do this, and that it was bad.

The term Psychic carried such a scarlet letter, and yet this is what I felt I was doing. So many of us that have stepped out into this way of thinking and being, have memories of tragic past lives. These lives hold memories where the punishment was so extreme and permanent. We were thought of as doing witchcraft, and death was the end result, usually in horrific ways. For me, all of this needed to be cleared out of my cellular memory before I could step out of my own fear.

My experience, as I grew stronger with communication, was one of healing, love, and beautiful messages. As I experienced this first hand, I knew there was no way this could be bad. Old Karma, anger, resentments, sadness and hurt wiped away in just one sitting with loved ones. Messages from Angels bringing insight, direction, a knowing that we are not alone, and that each of us has a purpose here. How could such healing be of the devil? People finding their Angels and opening up to them on a daily basis, feeling the love and guidance and making better decisions and choices for their lives, healing relationships and learning how to love again - this is God's work. This is not bad. It is beautiful and good.

I found myself feeling grateful, as I had the most amazing teachers along the way. Strong leaders in the Psychic community in my area, teaching me the right way to bring in my information. Knowing when someone has crossed or if they are stuck in between worlds. How to tell when an Angel is at my ear, or when it is a loved one that is saying hello. How to tell when it is my own higher-self bringing in the intuitive nudges. And so on. My Angels got me where I am today, through synchronicity and being at the right place at the right time, meeting the right people. I love them and hold them so close to me. My gratitude for their guidance in my life is infinite. I no longer live in the void of where I was before this journey.

Communicating with the Angels has been fascinating beyond words. They have shown me grand worlds outside of our own, using my mind's eye to bring in images of things I use to only read about in books or see on television. I am able to share messages with those around me from their Angels, and in doing so, seeing healing, clarity, and closure right before my eyes. Feeling the energy of the Angels as they wrap around us. There is no experience like it, and a most beautiful experience it is. This is an experience everyone can have and will have, when they are ready to open up to it.

It was in these experiences that I found I had a foot in both worlds. Often, I found it confusing to be between these worlds. One moment, I am feeling the unconditional love of the Angels and loved ones surrounding me. Then the next, I am experiencing the harshness of the world and reality I am living in. The intensity, demands, and expectations of my existence here on Earth, pulling at me and bringing me back down to "this reality." Anchoring me back into the grind of day to day life.

At times I would forget how easy it is to call in the love and the Angels around me. I would get caught up in the day-to-day grind, and the illusion that it will always be like this. The Angels were not going to leave me there though. They would send me signs and reminders that they were around. Soon enough, I would find myself shaking my head, and then moving back into a regular routine of meditation and communication with them. They would help me find my way back to the inner peace and to them.

Over time, this became easier and easier to do. I am not saying I am perfect at this by any means, but I sure do check in faster when I find myself in a bad mood, or experiencing something unpleasant in my world. It is as quick and easy as just thinking of something or someone you love, and then *boom*, you pull that love energy back into your reality, and soon all the bad things don't seem so bad. Everything I made so important doesn't seem so important anymore. All the upsets and anger subside. Peace is resumed, and I see a bigger picture at play.

The amazing part to me is, even with all my earthly commitments, the daily grind so to speak, the deadlines and responsibilities, the Angels always seem to have a way to get me through it. Showing me ways to find peace in a world that holds fear so closely. Shining a light where there is darkness, exposing the true nature of the action taking place.

The Angels often help me to see beyond what looks real, knowing that anything can change, and with love it will. Bringing me back to my peaceful place, even when I am having my very human experiences and reactions. Reminding me that I hold the power to create a better situation. Showing me where I hold my fear, and how at times, that keeps me a hostage in my own story. Reminding me that I have control over how much emotion I choose to give any situation. Where am I putting my energy? Is that the best use of my energy? What would I like to have happen instead? Helping me to become clear and to bring a better reality into my experience. This was a life changer for me.

I did find that over time, it became easier to create balance between the two worlds. To pull in my peace, when chaos is knocking on my door. To honor my feelings and disappointments along the way, as that is what I feel the human experience is about. To feel the feelings and have the experiences.

I love the fact that I have the gift of life, and with that, the gift to have these very experiences we so often complain about. Our world is rare. We get to do, see, and experience things here that are not offered anywhere else. To have the gift of not remembering where we came from, so we can move through our lives with the innocence of the first experience, as if we have never done this before; much like seeing things for the first time through a child's eyes. To take an adventure, and learn how to enjoy and love the adventure. To live life to the fullest, whatever that means for each individual. Life is a true gift.

We all hold so much potential, so much love, so much power in our own lives, and in the way the world looks to us. We all live in a world that supports us, and brings us the very things we are believing for. We are the creators of our realities. These realities we are creating are in fact the windows to our souls. The view to what is to come next.

What does your window tell you? Where does your soul want to journey next? What would you like to change? What would you like more of? This is the key to your life. Tell the story you desire. Spend time in that each day, and let go of the story filled with fear. Pull in your Angels, and ask them for their help in creating your desired story. Watch the magic unfold and the desired outcomes revealed. Keep the faith. It is coming to you now.

So I encourage you to call in your Angels. Learn how they feel when they are around you. Hear their whispers as they offer you guidance. They are here to help, to guide, and to bring you into your own peaceful reality, no matter what is going on around you. To know their love is to know you are love, and with love you can change anything, do anything, be anything. So go out into the world, and be Love. Put a foot in both worlds.

ANGEL KISS

LETTER TO YOUR ANGELS
Anu Shi Asta

This wonderful and simple technique of writing and receiving Angel Letters will help you communicate with your angels more clearly. You have an innate ability to channel messages from the Light and you can awaken this ability and enhance your intuition with this exercise.

Step 1: Opening

> Make yourself comfortable, light a candle, and play meditation music if that is helpful to your relaxation. Close your eyes and take a few deep breaths in and out. Sit quietly for a while and simply listen to your breathing. Imagine beautiful golden light filling your aura. This light cleanses your energy, protects you, and raises your vibrations. Ask Archangel Michael to give you extra protection, clarity, and courage. Imagine roots growing from the soles of your feet, grounding you deeply into Mother Earth. Be in stillness and bathe in the golden light until you feel peaceful.

Step 2: Your letter.

> Write a letter to your angel. For example: "Dear Angel, Please help me with _____. / Can you please tell me more about_____. With love, ____."

Step 3: Receive a letter

> Hold a pen and paper in hand. Let your angels know you are ready: *"Beloved angels and archangels from seventh dimension and higher. With an open heart I now ask to be an open channel for Angelic love and light. Please reply to me by using my hand, writing a clear message and answering all my questions. May it serve my highest good.*
>
> *So be it, it is done. Thank you."*

Be in stillness until you feel ready to receive. You may feel a shift in your hand or just an urge to begin writing an answer. You can also get into the flow of channeling, getting started by yourself. For example: *"Dearest _____ (name), I am your guardian angel. My name is _____"* etc. Soon, you will notice that the writing simply flows. Try not to analyze anything, just allow the words to flow. Wait until you are done to read and reflect on the message. Don't get discouraged if you only get one word or random lines or circles on your first time. The messages will become more clear as you practice.

Step 4: Closing

> Close your eyes and thank your Angels. Ask them to detach from your aura until you're ready to work with them again. Bathe in the golden light. Imagine the roots still firmly grounding you. Open your eyes and read your letter.

Talk to your Angels everyday either through writing a letter or simply sensing a question to your angels. They will always hear you and all prayers will be answered in a way that serves your highest good.

Know that Angels celebrate in Heaven every time you pray or think about them!

Chapter 11

Misdiagnosed

Gabriella Studor

It was a beautiful summer day. I recalled a memory of when my husband and I talked about having another child. As I brought this up in conversation, Dave happily agreed it was time to expand our family. We already had a handsome and very outgoing three-year-old son. His name was Brandon. We thought it would be fun for him to have a little brother or sister to play with.

Two months had gone by with no such luck in getting pregnant. I suddenly realized that the month we were in was "off limits." I explained to my dear husband what would happen if I was to get pregnant. I told him both our children would have birthdays in May. He looked at me with a weird look on his face. We both laughed it off and thought, *"What are the chances of that happening right?"* A few weeks later I began to feel dizzy. My intuition was telling me that I was pregnant. So I decided to take a pregnancy test. Two bars appeared right before my eyes. I was indeed pregnant! My obstetrician confirmed that our baby would be born in May, just like Brandon. I laughed as I told my husband. He also recommended I have a scheduled Caesarian section because with my previous pregnancy, I was not dilating and was in need of an emergency Caesarian surgery. Dylan was born on May 12th. He was beautiful and healthy! Dave and I were so happy and Brandon was very excited to meet his baby brother! Their birthdays were three days apart.

A few weeks later my body began to feel inflamed, sensitive to touch, and felt dull aches in my back. I felt chills throughout my body and my teeth chattered. I went to a medical clinic. They performed tests and found trace amounts of blood. They said this was normal after having a baby and that I was fine. I insisted that I was feeling awful and asked them to do further testing. They agreed to send out my test results to another lab. Within three days I received a call. The results indicated that I had a kidney infection so I was prescribed antibiotics. Sleep deprivation was taking its toll on me. I had difficulty concentrating and was very forgetful. I felt like a train wreck and would often cry. I was leaving a trail of hair wherever I would go. I was falling into a deep state of depression and I felt ashamed of how I was feeling. I thought I should have been happy after giving birth to our sweet baby Dylan.

I decided to make an appointment with my family doctor. He said what I was going through was normal after having a baby and that eventually it would pass. Months went by and I was feeling worse. I returned to see my doctor again and he offered to run some blood tests. My test results showed that I was anemic which he said was normal for most women. My hormones and thyroid apparently were in the "normal range." He could not give me an explanation why I was losing so much hair and why my menstruation had gotten so heavy. I asked him to refer me to an endocrinologist.

When I went to see her she examined my thyroid and said it was fine. I described all my symptoms to her and she decided that the best solution was to put me on the birth control pill. I left her office feeling like she just put a band aid on my health issues. A year went by with no improvement in my health. I stopped taking the birth control pills. I intuitively knew that was not the solution for me.

On one particular day, my whole life changed. We went for a nice walk with Dylan in his stroller and as a change of scenery, we decided to take a different path. As we were walking we noticed a sign advertising Angel Card Readings by an Angel Intuitive. The shop was called Serendipity. As we walked inside Dave suggested I get a reading. I went to the back of the shop and met Mindy, an Intuitive. As she started my reading, the dark cloud above my head began to lift. She told me I was going through a Spiritual Transformation. "Angel" Oracle card flew out of the deck, meaning I would be doing readings for others in the future. She told me I was a natural counselor and that many people would benefit from my guidance. "Gifts from God" oracle card also came up, meaning my psychic abilities were being developed, especially my clairsentience.

"Hello from Heaven" oracle card flew out and I gasped. My father who passed in 2006 came through in my Reading. I had no idea that this woman was also a Medium. She passed on the message that he wanted me to know that he spent time with the souls of my children before they were born. Also, the time I spent with him in the hospital before and during his passing brought him much comfort. Only then did it dawn on me that it had been three months after his passing that I conceived my son Brandon.

Weeks passed and I was guided to get another reading. There was a lovely woman at the store who was doing readings that day. She called herself "Amazing Di." She told me I was a Natural Healer, that I was to learn Reiki, and that I would heal myself, then later heal others. When I got home I told Dave about my reading and what I needed to do. We did some research and decided to learn Reiki together. I called the teacher the reader recommended and I signed us both up for the course. During the workshop, we were given a Reiki attunement. This process opens up your energy centers. It enables one to channel universal energy and helps to develop your psychic abilities.

The following day after receiving my attunement, I had a vision of my past life. I was shown exactly what had happened. In this vision, I walked up the stairs into a school. I had long blond hair and was wearing a white flowing dress. I was young. I walked through a hallway and to the other end of the school. I ventured out onto a beach, and as I looked back, I saw three young men having dark intentions. They began to chase me and I slipped and fell into the water. As a result, I drowned.

Another vision I had entailed a white horse galloping at fast speed, away from my friend's house during a snow blizzard. I made me feel quite uneasy. I asked my Angels what the vision meant and clairvoyantly I saw the knight of swords tarot card. It was a warning. Something hidden in my friend's home would soon be revealed. Shortly thereafter, I spoke to my friend about my vision. They discovered that there was black mold hidden in their basement walls which was causing many health issues!!

As my gifts developed, I had beautiful vivid visitations from my passed loved ones.

My father had come to visit me and we communicated without words. He stayed for quite a while, but hugged me before he left. In that moment I felt so much love and comfort. He was my guardian Angel watching over me!

One day I stumbled upon an earth Angel in disguise. He was a doctor who believed in treating the root cause of medical issues. He actually listened openly to what I was going through. Instead of accepting the norm, he took all of my symptoms into consideration and finally after six years, I got some answers. He prescribed natural supplements and bio-identical progesterone that was right for me. My body is now starting to heal!

My message to all who are reading this is to ask for guidance from your Angels. If something doesn't feel right, meditate and see what comes up. Ask them to help guide you and find the solutions to your problems. When you listen to their messages, your synchronicities will start to occur. Not only will you get your answers, but the right people, places, and opportunities will arise!

If you don't know how to contact your Angels, you can try this grounding exercise: Sit comfortably, imagine a beautiful glowing ball of white and gold light coming straight from your Angels over your head. Feel the light at the top of your head, moving down through your body, and out through your feet into the earth. Visualize a pink quartz crystal there, spreading energies up through your feet and into your entire body. Let it expand your energy. When you are done, imagine a zipper from the base of your spine and zip it up to your forehead. You are fully grounded, protected and connected to source!

ANGEL KISS

SOUL ANGEL

Josée Leduc

It's 5:30 am on what is supposed to be the first day of spring, but as I look outside I still see a small layer of snow covering the ground everywhere. I usually get up early so I can have time to write before the kids get up for school. Despite the fact that I had no intention of writing on this particular morning, I woke up with the sense that I was going to write regardless if I wanted to or not. As I was taking my shower, a storyline appeared in my head about angels and their purpose here on Earth. Even though I didn't want to, they wanted me to write a passage in this book. They kept on sending me information, flooding my mind with words and images, making it louder and louder in my head as I was trying to resist.

Flashes of a past event came back to mind: when I was ten years old, I was hit by an oncoming car while I was crossing the road. Even to this day, I have vivid memories of the event and I do recall seeing an Angel as I was regaining consciousness. Only my guardian Angel could have saved me that day from that horrific accident. My story might sound miraculous and it was, but it is also thrilling to see how one event can have such an impact on one's life. If it has positively impacted my life, it can certainly have a great impact on other people's lives as well.

The important thing you really need to know is that Angels really do exist. That is why they want me to continue helping them by writing about how Angels have helped me when I was ten and are still helping me today. They want me to tell you that Angels are all around us always. Sometimes, they show their presence by either whispering in our ears or by touching or kissing us on the cheek.

The problem is that often people are not listening or paying attention. Meditation helps to be in tune with the Angels. By meditating, our bodies, minds, and souls are in harmony. We can now receive messages or feel the Angel's energy beside us. Our soul is here living a human experience and human beings have forgotten the essence of who they really are. Thus, the purpose of the Angels is to help human beings to reconnect with their inner soul, because every soul has a special purpose on this planet.

LET THE ANGELS GUIDE YOU

LET THEM BE PART OF YOUR JOURNEY

BECOME THE LIGHT THAT YOU WERE MEANT TO BE

BECOME AN ANGEL WALKING ON EARTH

FORGIVENESS

Tracy Lacroix

I asked the Angels to send me a message to help me to forgive someone. Years had gone by, I thought I had moved on from this person until one day, I received a letter from him confessing that he took my gold locket that was to be handed down to my daughter on her eigthteenth birthday. He was asking for my forgiveness to clear his conscious so he could move on. I was so deeply hurt and didn't feel he deserved my forgiveness. I knew somehow I needed to let this go, I just didn't know how. This feeling of anger, resentment, and hurt consumed my thoughts for weeks. I tried to let it go through meditation, talking to friends, even writing out, but still the hurt would not go away.

One night, I lit some candles, got out my new deck of Angel cards and focused on healing myself so I could move on. I asked my Angels what I needed to do to stop this feeling inside me and forgive him. The first card I pulled read, *"To heal this situation, see the other person's point of view with compassion."* I sat with this card trying to understand it. I was frustrated! I yelled out, *"Okay Angels, how do you expect me to do that?"* I closed my eyes, took a deep breath, I felt my body being surrounded by light, my heart began to flutter, tears were streaming down my face. I felt a warm sense of compassion in my heart. I was told I needed to accept that there was nothing I could do, what's done is done. It was time to let it go. I was shown that he was truly sorry for what he did. I felt the angel's reassurance, comfort, and love around me.

As much as I wanted to be angry with him, I was able to forgive knowing that it must have taken a lot to admit what he did. I didn't want make contact to tell him he was forgiven so I asked the Angels what I needed to do. I continued to draw out cards from my deck. Each card I pulled connected to me in my heart, giving me messages that I needed to hear. I knew the Angels were speaking to me through my cards. I had a clear sense on how to move past this and other situations in my life.

I now use my cards daily to help connect me to my Angels, and to receive messages and guidance. They showed me that forgiveness and compassion is the key to moving forward in life. You need to feel it in your heart.

Chapter 12

Clearing Essentials

Gabriella Studor

Many people wish to attract love, joy, harmony, good health, and prosperity in their lives. Here are some helpful ways to achieve this.

Clearing Your Energies:

> You may clear your energies by safely burning White Sage, a Palo Santos Stick, Frankincense, or Jasmine incense which smells really nice! You can purchase these items at any Metaphysical store in your area. Light one up and wait until the flame goes out or blow on it until it starts to smoke. Make sure the smoke goes all around you and under your feet and above your head. Taking a sea salt bath is also highly effective. You may also call upon Angelic help. Say, *"Archangel Michael please cleanse my energies now. Remove anything from my auric field that's does not consist of love and light. Please infuse me with love, joy, and healing energy. Shield and protect me. Thank you, thank you, and thank you."*

Clearing Your Mind:

> Be mindful of your thoughts. Replace any negative thoughts or feelings with positive ones. You must also feel it and not just think it. So if you say, *"I am happy,"* you must genuinely feel the emotions of being happy. Being grateful for what you already have in your life will attract more blessings.

Clearing Your Body:

> Eat high vibrational food like fresh organic fruits and vegetables such as bananas, strawberries, blueberries and sweet potatoes. Eat protein from vegetarian sources such as lentils, beans, nuts and seeds. Drink plenty of fresh pure filtered water. Get enough sleep so your body is able to regenerate and heal.

Clearing Your Home:

>Getting rid of the clutter is one of the best ways to clear the energies in your space. Clearing items on the floor that are not serving a purpose. Get rid of old receipts, newspapers, books you no longer are interested in reading, etc. Go through your closet and dressers and donate, or give away items that don't fit or you don't love to wear. Dusting, sweeping, mopping the floors, and washing mirrors and windows are also great ways of cleansing your space. Use white sage, Jasmine, or any of the other items I listed to cleanse the energy in your space. You may open a window if you like while you're doing this. Your intention is to clear away any stagnant or heavy energy or anything that's not positive. Light the white sage then blow out the flame until it starts to smoke. This is called smudging. Make sure to first use sage on yourself to clear your energies. Start in the basement, if you have one. Then continue on the main level and start at the main entrance and move along the wall and go around every room and make sure you get all the corners and closed areas such as closets. Don't forget to do the center of the rooms also. When that's done, you can call upon Archangel Michael and ask him to fill your home with positive and loving energy. Don't forget to thank him! You can also visualize golden white light cascading in your entire home and filling it with love, joy, harmony, good health and prosperity. Ask Archangel Michael to stand at all entrances to your home such as doors, windows, or garage doors and to only allow beings of love and light or people into your home that have pure intentions towards you and your family.

Clearing Your Vibration:

>Your thoughts and emotions resonate on a certain vibrational frequency. Raising your vibration allows you to attract everything you want in your life such as a good job, a prosperous business, good health, wealth, joy and the list goes on. Your thoughts and emotions create results whether your vibration is high or low. If you are feeling emotions of guilt, shame, anger, or feel sorry for yourself, then you are vibrating at a lower vibration. If you are feeling emotions such as love, joy, compassion, and gratitude, then you are vibrating at a higher vibration. Like attracts like, so if you are feeling happy and lucky all the time then you will attract more happy and lucky situations. If you complain all the

time and feel like you have bad luck, you will attract more situations to complain about and attract more negative situations.

Make sure that you are making decisions when you are in a higher vibrational frequency!

How to Raise Your Vibration:

- Express Love and Gratitude
- Listen to classical or uplifting music
- Be around positive or fun people
- Spend time in nature
- Watch a funny movie
- Do something that makes you laugh
- Spend time with someone you love
- Play with your pets
- Be creative, draw, paint or make something

Positive Affirmations:

    I AM Love

    I AM Truth and Joy

    I AM Peace and Harmony

    I AM Kindness and Generosity

    I AM Gratitude and Appreciation

    I AM Present and Aware

    I AM Wellness and Prosperity

>I AM Compassion and Forgiveness

>I AM the Creation of Creator

If you want support, support others.

If you want love, love other people.

If you want to be heard, listen to other people.

If you want respect, respect other people.

Hope you enjoyed Clearing Essentials!

Compiled by Jewels Rafter

SECTION 3

HEALING

SECTION 3

Healing

Jewels Rafter

Divine healing involves an unexplainable act which resolves a physical affliction, emotional unease, or spiritual problem. Did you know there exists Angels solely dedicated to healing that are waiting to come to your aid? These Angels are with you right now. You simply have to ask them to assist you and they will be by your side in an instant, ready to heal your mind, body, and soul with their powerful celestial energy.

Although all Angels have the capacity to help us with healing and recovery, there is one Archangel in particular I like to call upon for energy, physical, or emotional healing. His name is Archangel Raphael and he has been referred to as the "Archangel of Healing" as his name is defined as "healer or medicine doctor" in Hebrew. When you request assistance from Raphael to heal a disease, a condition, or even emotional turmoil, the cure and the healing often occurs immediately. This Archangel patiently waits for people to provide him with permission to conduct his healing therapy. Occasionally some may even sense a gentle buzzing or vibrating energy around them as Raphael is sending healing vibes their way. But for other people, Raphael's healing is very subtle and gentle. Archangel Raphael can also assist you with reducing or eliminating pain stemming from short-term and chronic conditions. Again, this healing is a result of your asking for his help. In this manner, you offer your permission for him to intervene and heal the afflicted areas.

Healing however, starts in your mind and spirit. When you expand your awareness, your energy flows in a positive light. You become more open, more accepting, and physically healthier. You may even view yourself and the world around you with more compassion and understanding. You have more energy and are open to the possibility of healing. At this level of awareness, you have all the power you could possibly need to create a new reality: one of vibrant health and well-being. The mind is a powerful tool that can create well-being and happiness with a mere thought. If you remain open to the possibility of positive energy and loving intentions healing you, then you can experience the unconditional love and healing of your Angelic Guides.

Healing may take the form of Angels guiding us towards the correct vitamins or treatments that we require to eliminate disease or pain. They may highlight a story on the internet that is pertinent to questions you may have concerning your health and well-being. They may even align people who can support or counsel you to show up in your environment. The unconditional love and acceptance that derives from an Angel's energy is enough to heal even the most terminal diseases. I have witnessed clients with stage 4 cancer heal themselves with the assistance of spirit. I have watched people with chronic depression and anxiety find peace and happiness with the help of Angelic healing. Love is a very powerful healer. It can overcome almost any issue we have if we simply accept its loving energy. This is why Angels are such powerful healers. They emanate love and positive vibrations without condition.

I wanted to share another fabulous experience I had with one of my clients who was overcome with grief and physical pain:

She came to see me for a psychic reading and was in a very emotional state due to some traumatic recent experiences. After sitting down for thirty seconds, this lovely soul burst into tears. So I calmed her down with a box of tissues and a big hug, and with that, we started her reading…

We touched on a number of questions which were answered, but I could still feel that her energy was still very heavy and low. This poor soul had been to hell and back and she was absolutely drained emotionally and physically. She suffered from intense headaches and physical exhaustion. She felt that life was not worth fighting for anymore and her anger towards God and the Universe was so strong that she decided that she would NEVER pray or love anyone again. The loss of a loved one affects everyone differently, and in this case my client had built up walls of protection and isolation around herself as a protection mechanism. She had shut everyone out, even her Angels because for her, being close to others meant heartache, loss, and pain.

Throughout the whole reading all I wanted to do was wrap her up in the biggest bear hug and surround her with pink healing light to lift her spirits. She looked at me at one point and said, *"There is no Heaven. I am certain that there is only hell here on earth and this is all that exists."* I explained that we come to the earth plane to learn lessons and to grow from them, and in order to grow spiritually, the soul has to experience both positive and negative experiences such as the loss of a loved one. No one wants to lose someone they love under any circumstance. But then and only then, do we realize the true power of love and how it can break through any veil or barrier.

And as the words came out of my mouth, the lights in the room flickered and there, on the window pane, was a tiny white feather. We looked at each other and knew right there that an Angel was sending a message loud and clear: *"We are here to help! We are always around you whether or not you see, hear, or feel us."* This was their way of confirming that the Angels and our loved ones are always close by even in the afterlife. The energy in the room shifted and we felt a warm breeze engulf us. We both sat there with tears in our eyes and a smile on our faces. Once again, I was blessed with signs and confirmations from the other side or afterlife. Healing happens in many ways, and our Angelic Guides continuously wish to help us heal by sending loving energy our way. In that moment, I witnessed a shift in my client and healing had begun.

It's acceptable to grieve and mourn the passing of a loved one; this is part of the long healing process. But try to remember when the pain subsides a bit, that our loved ones are only gone from this physical plane here on earth. Love from the other side is so powerful that it breaks boundaries and limits. Be grateful for the opportunity to have loved someone with all your heart. Because in the end, experiencing real love is what it's all about. This is what drives the human spirit. So I urge you all, take a chance, go ahead and love your people with every bit of your heart and soul, and know that when their time comes, nothing will break the connection that love creates.

Angels and Guides derive from a place of unconditional love and send us healing vibrations with each message or sign they leave behind. If we allow ourselves to tap into that flow of energy, we open up the possibility of transforming darkness into light and sickness into health. All that is required is a little faith and a belief that we are healing.

ANGEL KISS

ARCHANGEL JOPHIEL
Kimla Dodds

So many angels to get to know! Did you know the prefix of "Arch" in Greek stands for "Chief" or "Ruling?" You may be familiar with the popular angels, for instance, Archangel Raphael who has powerful divine guidance for healing the mind, body, and spirit. Archangel Raphael is known for directing God's healing power to all living beings on planet Earth. Now Archangel Gabriel means "God's Hero" and is in fact God's special messenger. He is known for bringing announcements and news of upcoming events. He also helps us with all types of communication. Archangel Michael means "Who is like God." He is the most powerful angel mighty warrior and is God's enforcer of law and judgment. He protects all and is Mother Mary's constant companion. There are many, many more angels but there is one special Archangel that has a personal meaning to me. I am a Feng Shui Consultant and I love to ask Archangel Jophiel for guidance in creating clarity, balance, and beauty.

You see, Jophiel means "beauty of God." She inspires, enhances, and guides us to be more aware of the beauty that constantly surrounds us. She guides our thoughts in an uplifting fashion so we need not battle depression. She develops creative ideas and the willingness to explore the positive opportunities ahead. She also provides us with a glimpse into how beautiful our own hearts and souls truly are. Call her in to help release the harsh and ugly addictions that hold us back from enjoying our beautiful selves.

How powerful is Archangel Jophiel? She is an amazing and powerful leader. She alone directs fifty-three legions of angels and helps Archangel Michael to battle evil forces. A very bright yellow light surrounds her whenever she appears. A powerful torch she carries to burn negativity and to enlighten your beautiful path ahead. Call upon her to enhance your leadership and organization skills.

Archangel Jophiel loves to support students in their studies. Somehow her helping hand makes learning fun! She comes to the aid of artists, musicians, and dancers to bring art, grace, and sound so we can enjoy the finer things in life. She also takes great joy in creating the sound of laughter.

I personally have asked Archangel Jophiel to assist me with homes that need to find buyers. I call upon her to give that home a special new glow to attract the perfect souls for that space. By turning on all of the lights inside and out I feel her yellow light shining and working to clear unseen negative energy and emotional debris. Folks remark how lighter and prettier their home feels when I finish.

Beauty fulfills the soul! Make an intention to allow more beautiful experiences in your life. Reach out and ask my personal favorite Archangel, Jophiel, to protect, guide, and beautify your life.

ANGEL KISS

ANGEL OF PASSING

Wendy James

I worked in healthcare and was lucky enough to help many wonderful people at the end of their lives. I saw beautiful things during those experiences. When I first started I thought I was seeing things out of the corner of my eye. I would see a shadowy tall figure walk into certain resident's rooms, always the ones who were close to death. After ten years in this field, there was one constant in the rooms of the dying. There, standing in the corner, in the shadows and space was a loving presence, waiting.

After working with the dying, I realized that crossing over to the other side is as important as birth. It is a necessary transition to the next thing.

As time passed I really began to understand this patient shadowy Angel. I understood the importance of its role as an escort walking souls into the light. I also became aware of how misunderstood this particular Angel is and how feared.

Yet, in those moments, in those rooms with the dying, I found great comfort in knowing the patient one was there, cloaked in dark wings, to not be seen within the shadows and grey. I think it knew I was able to see it, or perhaps I wanted to think that it recognized my awareness of it. There was no interaction between this being and myself. No nods, or hellos. This amazing being was there for one reason; its focus remained constantly on the transitional soul.

I realized that this Angel waited and only watched. The love emanating from it, as it watched and waited, still stays in my heart decades later. This Angel has no power to change the course of things or affect the trajectory of the dying's journey. It seems to have no sense of time or need of it. Waiting is the only task until the transition occurs.

I grin now when I see portrayals of the Angel of Death as a frightening being and know it is not so. This is by far my favorite Angel: the compassionate, patient one who removes fear and confusion from our souls at the moment of passing. To have so much love that it can be given endlessly at such an important soul transition is a powerful roll.

I will never know if the residents that had passed during those times could see or feel it there too. I hope that they did. I hope that they found so much love pouring their way that fear was dispelled.

I had these experiences. I saw and felt how important this Angel's roll is. I still feel honored to have experienced each and every moment of those times. They changed me forever.

It was the first time I knew for sure that Angels do exist...

Chapter 13

Angels don't do stubborn

Roni Campbell

My story really begins when my partner of forty-three years was diagnosed with Vascular Dementia. This is not a fast progression disease, but is very hard on the person who has it, and the ones who love them. For four years, he fought this fight at home with me and with a specialist telling us there was nothing wrong. Then one day the magical day of nothing being wrong, transpired into them now telling me that he could not come home with me because it was not safe for either of us. They told me that he had to go to a Care Home facility. At that very moment, the world as I knew it fell out from under my feet. I was devastated to say the least.

I spent most days with him at the Care Home, volunteering to help with recreations as that gave me more time with him. He slowly became a shell of himself. Although he knew me most of the time, he was very angry because I would not take him back home with me. Yet I knew that he still loved me and that was enough for me. Amidst the challenging circumstances, I still loved him just as much as I ever did!

It was at this point that I made up my mind and accepted that I would spend the rest of my life alone. Yes, I was totally determined this was the way it would be. Little did I know that God and my Angels were not going to put up with my stubbornness. They had everything under control, except me.

To take my mind off what was happening for even a short period of time, I took up Beginner Square Dancing. I love to dance and was truly happy for the two hours my feet were flying to the music. I got enveloped by the music and the energy of the movement. It helped to get my mind off of the stress I was coping with on a daily basis. A year later, Tom came to one of my Club Dances. This lovely gentleman walked across the room and told me I had a beautiful smile. My response was, *"Thank you,"* and off I went without another thought. He had just moved to Kelowna and was looking for someone to spend the rest of his life with. I told him he would never find her hanging around with me!

At the time, I had no clue that this lovely man was going to save me in more ways than one. My partner was progressing into the final stages of this horrible disease, and it was becoming very difficult for me. During his episodes of dementia, I realized that he was spending time on the "other side," seeing his family in spirit and becoming comfortable as to where he was eventually going. What I did not realize was that he was not leaving the earth plane until he knew that I would be well looked after once he passed on into the light.

A few weeks later I hurt my back and I was confined to my couch for a month. My friend Tom phoned to ask me for coffee – not happening. I know now that it was my Angels that slowed me down so that I could get to know Tom. However I would not listen, so they put me in a spot where I had no choice.

After some time, we became friends and I was completely comfortable around Tom. He had just moved to Kelowna and was looking for "someone to spend the rest of his life with" he told me – but admitted that he was not looking at me that way! We were only friends. Little did I know, nor did I dream that the Universe had so much more planned for us than mere friendship!

Then one day, Tom admitted that he was falling in love with me. At 72 years old, I though? I felt a light energy flow through me and I finally realized that this love was supposed to happen. This was supposed to be part of the blueprint for the second half of my journey here on earth. The signs were clear, even my husband Johnnie approved of the situation. Every objection I thought of was dismissed; I felt that everything I had done the past seven years led to this moment. I honestly felt like I had been kicked in the stomach, the reaction was so strong. I was falling in love with him! A beautiful sense of peace came around me and I knew I would be all right. I finally heard and saw the signs from above. God and my Angels, as well as my partner, finally had me convinced. Johnnie had the Angels send Tom my way to be a part of my life. So that once he passed, I would be surrounded by love.

Tom and I were officially married on June 21, 2014 at our favorite lake. It was a simple and moving ceremony. Everything was absolutely perfect. I couldn't believe that at my age, love could happen again, let alone have love for two beautiful men in my life. I came back to the care home two days later to visit Johnnie and he came towards me, put his hands on my hips and asked smiling, *"Are you married yet?"* A month later Johnnie had to be moved to another facility, and only three months after the move, he passed away.

Signs that this was as it was supposed to be, that Tom and I were meant to be together continued to appear: Hawks showed up everywhere we went. A sign to me that Johnnie was watching over us. The final proof for both of us is that Johnnie did not pass until one minute after midnight, the day of Tom's Birthday. I believe it was a sign from my Angels proving to me that everything was as it was supposed to be.

Today, I feel blessed and happy to be surrounded by love. I thank God and all my Angels for their intervention to my stubbornness. They helped me to listen and to be open to beautiful possibilities for both Tom and myself. I also believe they worked though Johnnie by giving us his blessings and allowing him to leave the world in peace knowing that I was in good hands.

Compiled by Jewels Rafter

ANGEL KISS

A DIVINE PRESCRIPTION

Brian D. Calhoun

Angels and Guides of all sorts are always available to assist you. It matters not if it is finding a parking spot, stretching time, helping you to save money, helping with our healing, or something even bigger. They are truly our universal managers that we have employed to help make our life easier, more joyful along with protecting, supporting, and guiding us along the way.

You have Relationship Guides, Joy Guides, Happiness Guides, Financial Guides, Life Guides, Healers, and so many more. Today, let us bless you with an opportunity to work with a group of Guides that many underutilize, our Doctor Chemist Guides. This group is specialized in their fields having lived on the earth as Doctors, Surgeons, Chemists, and all things related to the body, mind, spirit, and emotions.

Here is a very simple nightly exercise to work with your Doctor Chemist Guides:

Each night before bed, get a glass of water to put beside your bed, and hold it in your hands as you state the following prayer, envisioning the water being filled with the perfect love, light, and energy for you.

Take a moment to call forth your Angels, Guides, Higher Self, and Doctor Chemist Guides. Ask them to infuse into the water throughout your sleeping period with what would best serve your highest good at this time, and would best support, nourish, and bless your body, mind, spirit, emotions, and your life with healing & improvement according to the divine will within. Take a moment to give your personal gratitude for all this and even better.

Now relax in bed with the awareness that they are now working with your complete energy system and bodies, throughout all time, space, dimension, creation, and reality. As you do so, you can also call in your other teams to do any clearing and releasing of all that no longer serves your greatest self, and imagine them coming in with housekeeping tools, and clearing your fields further of all debris.

It matters not if you stay conscious or not at this point, so take a few deep breaths and allow yourself to fall asleep.

When you get up in the morning, drink the water you had blessed throughout the night knowing that it has been filled with the perfect blend of vitamins, minerals, and energy perfect for you at this time!

Once you do so, take a moment or two as you are preparing for the day to give your own personal gratitude for all the beautiful blessings, treasures, miracles, and gifts of this day that are now unfolding in all areas of life.

Caution: Daily use of this healing tool will lead to greater happiness & health in all areas of life!

Angel Kiss

Surrendering to the Flow

Christine Gilmour

My name is Christine and I am a worrywart, or rather, I used to be! I was that person who overthought, overplanned, and relentlessly worried about almost everything. One area that plagued me was social gatherings. I used to spend days leading up to a social events going over all the details for before, during, and after each gathering. Of course some planning is important (for example, arriving on time), but not if one is so focused on the details that they are pulled away from the joy of the present moment. Once I invited the Angels to help me in my daily life, I found more peace flowing into my being and I was then able to surrender to the flow of life.

As a child, I had grown up hearing a little about Angels, such as the infamous Angel Gabriel sharing the birth of Jesus in the Bible. I would also read amazing miraculous stories of Angels interceding during life-threatening situations. It was not until I began reading books by one of my teachers that I learned they could also help us in our daily needs as well. Nothing is too big or small for them to assist us. They are literally just waiting for us to ask!

I discovered Archangel Michael who is particularly beneficial to call on when feeling fearful. For moments of anxiety, I wrote this prayer to help one move from anxiety to a more peaceful state, with the help of Archangel Michael. It is my hope you will find it a comfort in your time of need. Allow the words to wash over you, and bring more balance:

> *"Dear Angels, I am feeling worried and anxious. Archangel Michael, please scan my body and mind. Vacuum away any energies not in alignment with Love. Help me surrender the need to control and to focus on being Love. Help me to be right here, right now – focusing only on this moment. All I need flows effortlessly to me in divine and perfect timing. I am loved beyond measure. I am supported, protected and safe. Thank You!"*

Say this prayer as often you need to, to shift you from a place of worry to a place of peace. Like a newly exercised muscle, at first you may not see a change, but with time it becomes easier and you get stronger. I now have an unshakable assurance that no matter what life throws at me, the angels have my back. I have less anxiety and more joy. This is my wish for you.

Your angels are simply waiting for you to ask for help! So reach out to them and ask!

Chapter 14

Healing miracles with the angels

Michele Hanson O'Reggio

For Divine miracles, lean on God and your Angels for support.

For many years, I saw myself as a victim of circumstance. Even though I believed that life was inherently cruel, I also knew, in my heart, that there was a big purpose waiting for me. This galvanized my hunger to find the answers to pertinent questions, *"What is really going on? Why is this happening to me? What is my Life Purpose?"* What followed was a Divine journey that took me from darkness to light, eventually, revealing the Truth to me!

Along this journey, I experienced profound emotional, physical, and spiritual healing. One healer I met told me that I wasn't using all my gifts and that those gifts were a big part of my Divine Life Purpose. Another healer suggested that I should constantly affirm, *"I will, that there be light. I am light."*

In the midst of many Divine experiences, I had my first powerful encounter with the Angels. One night while I was laying wide awake, staring aimlessly in the dark, bright beautiful sparkles of light suddenly started appearing before my eyes. Awestruck and also confounded by the phenomenon, I knew that only the Angels could produce such Divine fireworks.

Thereafter, one morning, seemingly out of nowhere an email appeared talking about a course on Angel Cards which teaches how to receive Divine wisdom and guidance through them. I just knew that I had to take the course. Wasting no time, I immediately ordered my card decks.

When they finally arrived in the mail, I was thrilled! After all, Divine guidance had always played such a crucial role in my life and now I had this tool in my hands to truly hear the voice of the Angels through them. Even without any training, I had instinctively mastered the art of using them.

Who would have known that those cards would guide and support me through a terrifying gut-wrenching ordeal that was lurking around the corner!

One day, I pulled a card out of an Angels deck on romantic relationships. The message was to be aware of the red flags. I felt confused because a relationship was not my area of focus at that time. I shuffled again but the same card reappeared! Soon I came to know that a dear friend Sandra was severely ill again. Every now and then, Sandra had to undergo intense medical treatment for an extremely rare illness which very few people recover from completely. I felt engulfed by grief and guilt as I had spent a lot of time recently with Sandra while failing to notice anything out of the ordinary.

At that moment, I felt that Archangel Michael, the angel of protection, courage and strength, had guidance for me. I was told to forgive myself because I have done nothing wrong.

I also pulled out a card from the deck of Archangel Raphael, the healing Archangel, which told me alternate medical solutions were needed. I knew right away what this meant. We needed to contact the alternative healer who had helped with Sandra's recovery in the past.

This time again, he agreed to remotely provide the energetic and spiritual healing that Sandra needed while she underwent conventional treatment. However, he told us that this time her condition was alarmingly worse. Deeply saddened and aggrieved by this, I struggled to stay positive.

Every day, while Sandra was ill, I was guided to messages from the different decks that said positive thoughts produce positive results and there is sunlight. I really hoped this meant that Sandra would fully recover. However, fear and doubt would often creep in; could I really rely on these messages? After all, at that time, I wasn't formally trained in reading Angel Cards.

As the days went by, Sandra got progressively worse. I knew that the Angels are not allowed to interfere with our free will. They can help only when we ask them for help. Overwhelmed with frustration and a growing feeling of helplessness, I surrendered and decided to trust the guidance I was being given. Then, I received the messages to seek Divine guidance instead of worrying; talk to my Angels; and to look for alternate solutions.

I also pulled out a card from the deck on life purpose about animals with the picture of a girl on it. Knowing what it meant, I asked Sandra's Mom to give more attention to their cat who had been in distress ever since Sandra fell ill. This would aid in Sandra's recovery since animals are spiritually connected to their caretakers.

Then, through energetic dowsing, one of my healing practices, the Angels guided me to other natural healing modalities and healers from around the globe. Together, we created a powerful healing team at exactly the right time!

Shortly thereafter, I received messages from the Archangel Michael deck to let go of attachment to the situation; the problem is resolved; to release worrying and be at peace because all is well.

Archangel Michael also guided me to ask my dear friend, Michael, to visit Sandra and take her a gift that would lift her spirits up. Michael's presence in my life had also been divinely ordained as he had come my way through Archangel Michael's intervention. When I asked him to do the favor, he dropped everything and immediately went to see her.

He later told me that it was an honor for him to be on such a Divine mission, especially, since on his way to the treatment center, he noticed a truck with the words, "St. Michel," emblazoned on it. Incidentally, "St. Michel" is French for St. Michael. Eventually, Michael's visit with Sandra turned out to be an exceptional gift as he was able to glean insights that were meaningful to her recovery.

Shortly thereafter, I received messages from Archangels Michael and Raphael that I'm on the right path and to expect a miracle. Ecstatic to hear the news, I kept marching forward on this healing mission!

The Sun and The Final Healing

One day, as I was looking out of my window, I felt fixated and totally enthralled by the sun. Later on, I learned that it was one of the hottest days in history. I had a gut feeling that Sandra's recovery had begun. A message from the deck of Archangel Michael told me of new beginnings and a fresh start.

That day, as I entered the treatment center, I heard a voice singing Celine Dion's, "A New Day Has Come" - *"I can't believe I've been touched by an Angel with love. Let the rain come down and wash away my tears. Let it fill my soul and drown my fears. Let it shatter the walls for a new sun. A new day has come."* The words were coming out of Sandra's mouth, yet it was too intensely BEAUTIFUL and sweet for any human voice to possibly sing.

My heart melted and my soul was entranced as my eardrums absorbed that Divine rendition. Words won't do justice to describe what I was feeling in those glorious moments but it should suffice to say that I could clearly feel the presence of God's Angel who was singing through Sandra!

Although she hadn't completely recovered, in that moment, she appeared to be completely at peace. Her physical suffering was almost inconspicuous. I remember noticing a soft warm glow around her as if she had been touched by the wings of an Angel. Sandra would later tell me that indeed she often saw Angels in her room - bright sparkles of light and mist swirling around her.

When I went home that night and opened YouTube, a video with the words, "New Day," and a picture of the Sun immediately started playing. Finally, I knew that we had reached the point of victory previously indicated by the card messages related to the Sun.

A new day, it certainly was because we had finally received the miracle - Sandra was healed despite the fact that almost no one with her rare condition ever recovers fully or as rapidly as she did. It took her only four weeks to return to good health. Whereas, in the past, the illness had kept her in its clutches for more than five months.

Later that night, I received messages on life purpose. I was told to follow my heart's true desires and to make a decision. Also, that I am angelically guided, supported, and protected as my heart's desires and dreams become a reality!

I am very grateful for the miracles I have experienced and these are my words of gratitude to God and the Angels:

> "Through the years when everything went wrong
>
> Together we were strong
>
> Through the years
>
> You've never let me down
>
> You've turned my life around
>
> The sweetest days I've found
>
> I've found with you...
>
> You've kissed my tears away."
>
> - "Through The Years" by Kenny Rogers

ANGEL KISS

MAKING SENSE OF LIFE

Barbara Grace Reynolds

I was thinking today about my life and all of the things that have occurred. I can remember when I was back in my 20's and taking a psychology class in college. I came home for a weekend visit and spent most of the time telling my parents about everything they had done wrong in raising me. And I knew that I was right! I have had two marriages and each one felt like a bad choice but I did them anyway. After all, I am so intelligent! Smile. I thought my marriages were based in undying love; now I know that they were based in my fears about proving that I was a good enough person to be loved. Here I am now, almost sixty years old and finally learning what life is all about.

What has helped me to learn are the beautiful Angelic Beings whose guidance I now accept. It took me years of making the effort to be consciously connected with my Guidance and following their advice, but now I can look back over my life and see how everything that has ever happened really does make sense. They showed me how, even when I wasn't aware of their Guidance, they were guiding me. This is the reason that my marriages never felt like really good ideas. Perhaps if I listened, my life would have been different!

I know that the reason I have these revelations now is that I am no longer looking to see what is wrong or to take things personally. It's amazing to realize that no one was ever really against me. Even those people that I felt were not on my side have been a huge benefit in my life. Their pushing at me has helped me to move in ways I would not have moved. They have helped me to see beliefs that I would not have seen. They have helped me to create a life that I can actually love and enjoy. It all makes sense now.

I would like to take this opportunity to say to anyone that has been a thorn in my side. Thank you, for helping me to finally see the Truth of who I am. Thank you, for pushing me so that I had to look within myself for the Guidance and support that is there. Thank you, for shifting me out of victimhood into a woman who stands in her power and knows her value.

Everyone I have ever had any contact with has been a part of my evolution and growth and I am grateful to each and every one of you. ***Thank you!***

Chapter 15

Inspirations

Jennifer Del Villar

As I sit here, close my eyes, and try to see myself with the periscope of several years passed, it would be as if I was looking upon the horizon at a distant sailing vessel that truly was just a speck upon the sea. In much gratitude for learning that occurs by living, I would never in a million years have imagined I'd be where I am now; but I am. I live in the present, treasure the past, and dream for the future. The emphasis is truly on living fully today, this very moment.

I think I always believed in possibilities and knew instinctively that I was not alone. I knew all beings are connected and truly call forth solidarity. My parents were a huge influence on me in differing ways (Mom was the spiritual artistic dreamer and Dad was the steady responsible rock). I rebelled at times to my intuition and the truth that I now embrace; but I always "knew." When I allowed myself to trust my inner instincts and acknowledge what my gut was telling me, that is when I "met" those that have guided me both silently and not so silently. My Guides are treasured friends, angels, and souls. They nudge me, they validate my thoughts, they allow me solace and comfort in their presence in both good and "growing" times. I can always trust them to be within reach at any given moment if I just return to my calmness, heart and spirit. I have also had the privilege of "feeling" souls that have been in my life and have moved on from this realm to transform into their next adventure. I notice them in the fragrance of a remembered scent that drifts gently through a summer breeze or perhaps as a tingle that awakens the hair on my neck in a peaceful and loving way or in a playful moment in a dream.

I cannot express the impact of the blessing of my incredible circle of lights surrounding me that are physical beings here - including a wonderful musical tribe; I would also not be where I am without my earthly family, friends, and tribe. I would be negligent to mention the souls still on this earthly plain who have transitioned to another space away from my current experience. Those are individuals who have made incredible impacts in my life, but where the journey of friendship, love, or any combination has propelled us away from each other into different directions. We reconnect in a different way to check upon each other; again some meet me in my dream world. While the parts we played in each other's script may be completed for now; they fulfilled a purpose. I know that there are some who have had relationships and events that have brought about horrible consequences; instances where it's really a situation where "we" pull ourselves from the ashes into the light. But, in speaking only from my own experiences – as tough and horrifying as they may have been for me – they have also been incredible catalysts into beauty.

So to paint you a picture of "how" and "what" I see, it's basically this: I open my heart and believe in the teachings of the great masters of the earth, and to me "God" is universe itself, which is mighty and all encompassing. But I also live with beings of vibrational light and energy that I connect with on a very personal level. I feel them within my heart and can touch, talk, play, find comfort in, and just share quiet moments together sitting in a beautiful space with a grand path and meadow out in front. My "little family" comes in the form of an Arch-Angel, a Goddess, tree spirits, and animal totems. There are also other travelers that visit on occasion (when I allow and open the door); however, my "little family" are my constants.

My "little family" has opened doors to the courage to be who I am meant to be and allow me to continue to skip merrily along the path to do what I feel beckoned to do. And thus, I am a life transformed; I think ultimately knowing I'm not alone and I'm allowed to embrace, know, and live authentically as myself in the circle of the dance of my life. I've always been a creative, intuitive, empathic soul and at the same time have been a dichotomy - a little "unique" but with the ability to fit into almost any situation (mainstream or not) as well. At times that confused me – and I think I hid a part of myself away to be what I considered "normal." What the heck is normal anyway? But today I embrace my trifecta world. A mainstream career, embodiment into the spirituality of the universe, and living my deepest passion and bliss which is song, the written word and the voice.

I have, and still face, patterns of saying "yes" when my instincts are telling me – "NO!" I lean sometimes towards "wanting" to be in control over a given situation; but stop and allow myself to be still and let universe to do what it needs to do. So, in the presence of my beloved "little family" I now see the patterns as they raise their hissing cobra like heads and ask for guidance and assistance in allowing those patterns to leave into the beauty of the universe with love and light.

So as to what I would paint for you to inspire you to look within, which is my hope, I'd say this: As we look upon our past, there will be things that we questioned "why," "how," "really?" – "oh no - that's not me." Be gentle with yourself, toss away gently the shame and the guilt, and trust it was in your existence for an incredible reason. When we shed the gift of the tethers, cages, traps, and expectations that were there for a purpose at a given time and allow ourselves the freedom to simply be - ideas and outlook shifts. It is amazing how the sky is bluer, the clouds are fluffier, and everything seems clearer. It's a feeling of coming out of the winter of deep reflection to experience a new breeze that whispers of love and light.

If a thought pings in your mind that focuses on faults and defeat; thank them for the transformations they may have allowed, and ask them gently, graciously, and lovingly to leave you. Vision them as dandelion seeds ripe for freedom that float delicately away on the wind. I would then invite you to fill that renewed open space with words that speak to the magnificence of you. Let those powerful visions shine and vibrate deep within you.

EMBRACE LIFE! It is a series of magnificent moving pictures. Allow the camera of your soul to process and illuminate each experience fully; let the screen reveal the journey to true self and true purpose. The universe will always show it to you if you only ask. Be quiet in moments to reflect on that which you'd find the most amazing of adventures (and the adventure is yours - it could be spending time beautifully with the ones you love, making a gracious meal, or performing on a stage to thousands); it's all exactly as it should be – trust that. Truly know to the depth of your core what that looks like for you - see it, feel it, know it.

I'd also remind you beauties that life is cyclical and there are moments where again winter is needed to bring forth the growth of change. So don't be disappointed if you find yourself journeying from one seasonal cycle to the next in your life; it is necessary. But, having shed those tethers, you'll hopefully have a better understanding of those seasons and embrace them as glorious gifts of times, of reflection, and going within rather than unwanted nuisances. It's all a growth process, a process of rebirthing us forward to ourselves and our purpose. We are like bulbs that grow into beautiful tulips, we bloom, shine, rest in the momentary "death," regrow and bloom again.

As I said before, for me looking at "me of the past" is like looking at a distant horizon. But what a beautiful road it has been, the road ahead has a rainbow's arch and the now is filled with delight. You are never alone – they are here with you – we are here together – we are one embodied in different forms, but yet a tribe that holds strong in a brilliant magnificent embrace of energy. May you know how loved, worthy, brave, incredible, magnificent you are and may you always allow the radiant light vibration to shine from you into the world to create a truly illuminated and empowered space.

As I tell my children; I love you like a circle – it NEVER ENDS! Muahhhh!

Compiled by Jewels Rafter

SECTION 4

DIVINE INTERVENTION

SECTION 4

DIVINE INTERVENTION

Jewels Rafter

The dictionary describes divine intervention as "a term for a miracle caused by a deity's active involvement in the human world." In layman's terms, this describes the phenomenon where Angels intervene and save humans from life or death situations, then disappear without a sign. This happens more often that you may realize. You see, I've been offered proof of Angels' existence at regular intervals in my life through experiences so profound they've given goose bumps to atheists. These epiphanies have draped me with an inner peace, washing away my fears, and giving me hope for the future. The intense happiness I feel during these occurrences eventually dissolves and I fall back into a safe complacency again. As time passes and everyday life gets in the way, I start to reminisce until yet another unexpected collision with the celestial hits me and replenishes my faith. I know we are protected, as the proof we're given is unexplainable, yet it remains vividly engrained in our minds like an imprinted image. However, human's appetite for miracles remains insatiable and like moths to flame, we crave more stories of miraculous interventions.

As a child in the mid 70's, I can recall driving in the car with my mother during the winter time. It was a bright, sunny, wintery day and the roads glistened with icy conditions. During this era, wearing seatbelts was only a suggestion and not an imposed law and I clearly remember bouncing around the front seat of the big Impala without a care in the world. I sat untied and looking out the window at all the trees along the highway, as we sped down the road, radio playing in the background. As the music played, I sang along to the tunes and belted out the words "slow down" along with the artist in the song. This was the first sign from our Angels to pay attention to our speed. As we came around the off ramp on the highway, the car began to swerve back and forth and fishtail. I was sure we would hit the car in front of us. But somehow, the car managed to straighten up and miss the other vehicle we were sliding towards. Minutes later we were back on the highway heading home.

The small incident behind us, my mother stepped on the gas pedal and off we went! All seemed reasonable for the next fifteen minutes or so. Then out of nowhere the car hit a patch of black ice at high speed and started to spin around 360 degrees. My mother had lost complete control of the car. It kept spinning in circles and heading towards the ditch directly in line with a huge oak tree. We glided full speed towards the tree and I went flying down to the floor of the front seat. My mother yelled and I was certain we were in trouble and that death was imminent. I remember saying to myself, *"Angels please save us. I don't want my Mommy to be hurt."* Instantly, the car stopped merely inches away from that very tree. I immediately felt a warm sensation across my shoulders as though someone had put their arms around me to console me. I believe my Angel had wrapped her wings around me as protection.

We sat there in shock for what seemed like an eternity. Minutes later, a car stopped on the side of the road to make sure we were safe. A gentleman with a gentle demeanor walked over to us and asked if anyone was hurt and if he could help in any way. My mother thanked him and told him we were fine, just a bit shaken up by the whole incident. Seconds later out of nowhere, a tow truck emerged to help remove the car from the ditch. Cell phones did not exist back then, so we were perplexed at how they knew we were stuck at that very location. Nonetheless, I thanked my Angels for coming to our aid and told my mother she drove way too fast. She laughed at my comment and wrapped her arms around me telling me she was so happy I was not harmed in the accident. Whatever you refer to as your higher power, embrace that there is something bigger out there than we realize.

Most will agree that by definition a miracle is some kind of perplexingly impossible incident not explicable by natural or scientific laws. It is an event that leaves a rather large question mark in the minds of those who observe it. For some, it may shake the foundation upon which they stand, beckoning them to question their entire outlook on reality; while for others it is dismissed without further contemplation as pure chance or coincidence; something "totally scientifically explainable."

Occurrences like these happen quite frequently; where a person facing a life and death situation is guided internally by something of a higher source that leads them out of imminent danger. An outside observer looking at the situation wouldn't necessarily see anything divine or miraculous about the occurrence. But to those directly experiencing the phenomenon, this guiding presence is unmistakably real and completely undeniable.

I have heard of situations where people were in imminent danger or faced with life or death situations, then unexpectedly, at the peak of their emotional distress, emerges a completely different sensation. An unexplainable inner voice or higher power leads you to safety. It is my belief that in these circumstances, our Guardian Angels step in to assist.

Humans have the ability to experience the intervention of something beyond this dimension right through our own body and mind. Changes in mental perception, sudden intuitive movements of the body, or a cognitive "download" of information pertinent to an emergency situation at hand are all examples of Divine Angelic intervention.

During emergencies or when we are in danger are the only occasions where Angels or Celestial Guides will intervene on our behalf. This phenomenon occurs when we are faced with our own mortality. It forces us to have blind faith in something we don't necessarily comprehend. As a result, people are forever changed and filled with gratitude as well as an unnerving sense of peace and serenity.

If you have been blessed with an unquestionable miracle, be sure to thank your Guardian Angels for intervening and for protecting you from harm. Gratitude goes a long way and may just reinforce your relationship with these Divine Beings.

Makes me ponder...perhaps cats aren't the only ones with nine lives?

Compiled by Jewels Rafter

ANGEL KISS

DO YOU BELIEVE IN ANGELS?

Deb Bergersen

I do now!

Growing up, Angels were not a part of my everyday life or beliefs. There is an old saying that says something like: "You have to grow older to be wiser" or "Wisdom comes with age." That is what happened in my life where angels are concerned. In fact, I was nearly sixty when I realized what a part my angels have played in my life. I know as a child there were people who talked about angels or guardian angels but it wasn't something that I had any strong feelings about one way or another. As I review my life, I find there have been several times when Angelic forces have intervened to help me.

The first time I remember this happening was when I was sixteen years old. I was with my mom and oldest brother's family for an Easter break in California to visit my younger brother. We went to the beach as it was a beautiful warm and sunny day, perfect for a swim in the ocean. My niece and I had just waded in to about waist deep and were fooling around in the water. Suddenly I heard her yell for help. I started trying to swim towards her as I was the closest to her. The next thing I remember was realizing I was in trouble too.

I kept thinking, *"Okay, this is it. I am going to drown."* All the while wondering, *"Is my life was going to play out in front of me like a movie?"* I don't remember seeing any movie or anything that dramatic. I looked out at my niece and felt so sad. If I could not reach her from where I was how was she going to be saved? Then everything went blank for me. My younger brother reached my niece. Somehow he knew that she needed help. I woke up on the beach spitting water and coughing. I had a guy over me I had never seen before. The lifeguard on duty had ran out and pulled me in. My first words were to check on my niece. She was in trouble and needed help. That's when I found out she had already been pulled to safety.

I had swum in the ocean before. It was an exciting experience for me. However, I didn't know until that day what the riptides could do if you were caught in one. The harder I tried to swim out to my niece the more the riptide caught me and pulled me farther out to sea. I learned a valuable lesson that day, and knew that Divine intervention had saved me.

My Angels were watching out for me and thanks to them I am still here today.

Angel kiss

Falling Angel

Maureen Sullivan

I believe that when you receive a pass in life, a profoundly different path presents itself, not only to teach you the beauty of life and open you up, but to challenge it. You are strong enough.

I believe I had experienced such an event at the age of six.

It was shortly before Christmas and my siblings and I were playing in a field in my backyard. We lived in what probably felt as a child, a rural community with open and tree filled fields.

In the field, off the path, there also were industrial sized sewers that had been placed in the ground sometime earlier that year which were fairly deep and concrete. One particular day, I stepped off the path and fell into one of the open sewers. I awoke at the bottom of the sewer looking up to my brother whose tears I could feel falling down on me. I fell and landed with my head gently cradled in my arm. I can still clearly see it in my mind. When I was rescued from the pit and medically tended to, I had just broken my arm. I don't think at the time, I questioned why I hadn't hit my head on the bottom of the concrete, or why I had fallen cradling my head. It wasn't until I was an adult, in my dreams or a part of my awakening, remembered the sense of having my head cradled in gentle loving hands as I was falling. I just knew that my Guides were watching over me and helping me fall.

Shortly after that experience, we moved to England, where as a child, I discovered how sensitive and energetically open I was. It was as though a piece of me broke open so that the light could come in. I became curious about spirits and Angels asking my friends questions about these divine beings. Yet I was not conscious of why I was so certain. One day in the big house we lived in, I was visited by a woman holding a lantern that to me, felt like an Angel of light. She shone a bright yellow light into the room where I slept. I wondered if perhaps that she was the one that helped me gently fall that day.

It would be years later as an adult where a well-known psychic and medium would share with me, that this experience was a pass and my

Guides were there protecting my little body as I fell. It wasn't my time to leave the earth yet! Although unaware at the time, I feel this experience was a precursor to many signs and blessings along the way in my life. I am blessed and grateful.

CHAPTER 16

THE POWER OF ARCHANGEL MICHAEL
Kimla Dodds

Looking for a parking spot in the pouring rain on a crowded University campus is like trying to shop for a pair of best fitting jeans at closing time, frustrating! After more than a few turns around the block, I finally did find one on the opposite side of the building where my Interior Design Class about to begin. Running through the downpour, soaked, and breathless I entered quickly. I loved being a part of the synergy that engulfed this classroom.

When my professor asked to see me after class I was a bit reserved as to the intention. We reviewed my assignments and she seemed very interested in my talent. Talk turned to the different styles of designing and she asked me if I had ever heard of Feng Shui? My inner voice was screaming, *"Is she asking me to decorate a Chinese Restaurant?"* When she informed me I had an instinctive feel for the flow of a room, and may enjoy learning Feng Shui, I exhaled. Teachers sure do have the power to influence our minds at times. I immediately began a search and journey that would change not only my life but also many others.

It was a pivotal year, 1998, when I located the first Chinese Feng Shui Class coming to the States. How blessed I was to attend the premier seminar with Grand Master Lin Yun in San Diego, CA. Having my eyes wide open, I accepted the sacred responsibility of helping to shift other's energy through "The Art Of Placement" as Feng Shui is called. I was admitted to a year of apprenticeship study. It was in those twelve months that my childhood psychic abilities reached new levels. Studying under a Chinese Master provided discipline, insight, and deep daily meditations. Thirsty and inquiring minds of students ask questions that were not answered in words. We were told to go back and meditate. The answers will appear. Before long, with slight concentration I could tune in and visualize the floor plans of my assignments. The house came to life and I was able to feel myself walking through them, just like I was there in person walking through the front door. The knowledge came immediately where to place the furniture. I also felt the flow and blockages of Chi, lightness and darkness, warmth and cold, trapped emotions, and could hear harsh arguments that hung in the air. Space clearing was the last of my studies to end my life changing year as an apprentice. Feeling worthy and confident,

I started my Feng Shui practice.

Within a few years, Feng Shui became more popular and my clients found me by word of mouth. I received a call from a friend of a friend located in New York. She was beginning a home renovation and was interested in getting a Feng Shui Consultation. Having family and friends in New York, I was delighted to fly in and combine business with pleasure. I accepted her request. Informing her of a few details I needed to get started, we confirmed her date and time. She sent over her floor plan, I placed it on my home altar and began to meditate. In seconds, the house came to life receiving visuals through my third eye. I was standing in the front door and looked down to notice oak wooden floors, to my right was a cluttered dining room and outdated window coverings. To my left was an unoccupied den with large scale chairs and a massive TV that was blaring as if to reach out to someone upstairs.

Walking down the hallway, I turned into a small, closed off kitchen. I began to feel shortness of breath. I knew right away that this was the reason the lady of the house wanted to renovate. The kitchen needed to breathe and wanted to be opened up to the flow of the home. My mind's eye walked me up the staircase to the first bedroom on the right. That's when it hit me. A very heavy dangerous feeling of being held, manipulated, and a sense of drowning came over me. I tuned in deeper to see a young teen age girl dressed in black Goth attire with safety pins in her ears, black nail polish, and very black long hair.

She wore jeans and work boots and held something shiny in her hand. It was a razor blade and as she walked in to the dark bedroom closet she began cutting herself on her arms. I could feel a very dark low vibrating ball of entities rolled into a massive negative being residing in there. This conglomerate of evil had her hypnotized. That's when I confirmed an entity removal and space clearing had to take place before any enhancing Feng Shui could be done.

The next week I arrived into JFK airport and I was greeted by my own family members. My task ahead was to speak to my client before consultation day. Family set up a cocktail party and invited my client as she was a mutual friend. When she walked in I could see a tall male spirit walking in behind her. My client was a very attractive conservative blonde wearing a tailored brown pants suit. The spirit behind her told me he was her father and he was also wearing a distinctive 1940's brown wool suit with hat in hand. He telepathically joked that they didn't plan to dress so similar. I smiled and reached out my hand to her not mentioning our uninvited guest now standing to the right of her. We found a private corner and began to talk. She was very excited about sharing all of her ideas and future plans for the new and improved reconstruction.

I took a deep breath and explained my psychic abilities. Then I went on to describe her home to a tee. Her eyes became wide and interested. She was very impressed with the detailed description and immediately ordered a strong cocktail. The hostess was very accommodating! Explaining a bit more on how this process of energy shifting works, I shared the basics of space clearing, and how removing the unseen blockages will allow a better Chi flow throughout the home. Then I quietly described her teen age daughter. I held her hand as I recounted what I had experienced. Her hand flew up to her mouth as she gasped and said, *"No one knows that, only me and our priest."* I comforted her and asked if tomorrow, instead of beginning the Feng Shui as planned could we remove the dark energy in the bedroom closet? *"Yes, please help my daughter,"* she whispered.

Having gained her permission, I invited another informed family and friend to accompany me on the clearing session. Awakening early to meditate, I dressed, wearing a rosary and holding holy water, sage, and Himalayan Salts in my hands. I prayed to Archangel Michael, the Archangel of protection, to protect me and guide me as I became determined to help this family. We arrived to the address and I chuckled as the house looked exactly as I had pictured it. Even the TV was still blaring in the den. A photo frame sitting in the bookcase lit up and I asked the lady of the house if that man in the photo was her father. She answered, *"Yes, but I never knew him. He passed when I was an infant."* I then shared his visit at the cocktail party. She laughed at his sense of humor and was grateful in knowing he was around her.

Before we started, I requested all doors remain open while we are in clearing session. Making sure that only the lady of house, myself, and our friend were the only people in the house. I lit the sage and ascended the staircase. The lady of the house stood by the opened bedroom door, my friend was standing at the side of the bed. I walked in and opened the bedroom closet door, turned on the light and loudly prayed to Archangel Michael. *"Help me to remove this energy from this house Archangel Michael,"* I pleaded. That's when my shoulders felt two huge hands holding me still and I became a strong, straight rod of steel. Then a white light came blasting out of my solar plexus like a Star Wars laser filing the closet with a radiance of pureness. I heard myself say, *"Be gone from here now!"*

A creepy voice you would hear from a Halloween movie replied, *"No, I have been here a very long time."* Then the light extending from my stomach began to pulsate and turn blasting even more powerful light energy than before. I reached for the rosary cross hanging around my neck and the entity came forward charging directly through me knocking me to my knees. I looked to find my friend standing bedside, mouth wide open and her hair flying as it went passed her. The lady of the house fell into the bedroom door when it exited. Then we heard the front door slam shut. A nauseous feeling came over me as I tried to find the strength to speak. In a flash Archangel Michael picked me up and I was standing on my feet. The beam subsided and his hands let me go. I'm not sure which one of us exhaled first but it was obvious the dark energy was gone. We were elated!

Immediately, the room was lighter, brighter, and a bit glittery when I scanned the space. My heart was still racing and I was left with an overwhelming exhaustion that is hard to describe. Archangel Michael then suggested I lay down for a bit. I nodded in agreement and said not to worry the house was cleared. That evening I received a phone call from the lady of the house. She was so happy she thanked me again and again. Her daughter came home from school and asked to go to the shopping mall with her mother. She said wanted to look for a new bedroom comforter. When she came out of her room, she had taken off the black nail polish, no more safety pins in her ears and she was wearing white! Can you believe they came home with a new comforter, one with angels all over it! Am happy to report this teen age girl is grown up now and has a loving daughter of her own.

I am so blessed to be able to be of service through this work. We are all so grateful for the power of Archangel Michael. He is always there when you need him. Please call upon him in your hour of need to protect you and guide you. He requires your permission to come in to work with you. Give him permission! He is the most powerful Archangel and his job is to protect and never leave the Blessed Mother's side. But he can be in more than two places at once. So call out his name and watch for his arrival. You know angels are around us always. I'm so happy to know we are never alone.

Miracles do happen, to people just like you! May the angels protect you and guide you and yours always.

~ Many Blessings, Kimla

Angel kiss

Do Angels Intervene?

Deb Bergersen

Angels were not something I grew up believing in, yet as I grew older, I questioned them and asked for their help. Angelic support has shown up in many ways in my life. When I finally figured out how much they were present and learned to invite them in, I found that they were eager to offer help with support and guidance. As I continued to learn about Angels and Guides and how they could help us, I decided to try a few experiments to see if it they would help me too. Guess what? It worked! Many would tell me that I could ask for all kinds of help and they would answer. So I started experimenting with parking spaces at local busy stores. Funny thing was that once I started, the parking spots were always available when I arrived. I made other small requests which sometimes showed up immediately and other times a bit later. Yet I always received their answers and help.

When my answers do come in, I give thanks for their assistance each time. It also seems that they delight in leaving me small tokens to let me know they're around me. For this I am grateful as I know they have my best interests at heart. My Angels and Guides must really enjoy making me put the pieces of their puzzles together; they provide small parts, that hopefully will all come together and make sense to me down the road. It seems that each piece is given one at a time until they all fall into place. They spent many years going unnoticed. But now they leave me small feathers, rainbow clouds, and hearts everywhere. The sight of a special bird can even be my sign that they're near!

I started awakening several years ago to voices or smells and feelings of someone being close by. Most of the time they were a warning me of something that could cause me or my family harm. A few times now it has been the smell of propane or natural gas. The last time I smelled something, it was starting fluid for a car. With their assistance, I could be forewarned when something was wrong in the house and take the necessary precautions.

Luckily for me, I have had many instances where proof has been given of their existence and loving care for us, their humans. To any who question this, I challenge you to look back over your life at the times when you have been "lucky" or "saved by a small delay," chances are you will find Angelic intervention has shown up in your life too!

ANGEL KISS

CROCKPOT STORY

Helen Cline

I had just walked away from my computer and was entering my kitchen, when I walked right into a wall of warmth. The warmth had a kind of shape and encompassed about the size area of an adult person, only maybe taller. I moved my hands around and could feel where the warmth stopped and started; it did not have an exact shape but was more a defined area.

I went back to the computer and messaged my friend I had just been chatting with. I described what I was sensing and told my friend, *"There is someone standing in my kitchen."* She told me that in her experience, warmth meant an angelic presence.

While we were going back and forth about what this could be or mean, I felt a warmth about the size of a wide bracelet encircle my forearm. This bracelet sized area was moving up and down my arm. I told my friend I thought someone was trying to pull on me. I decided if someone was trying to get my attention I should try to figure out what they wanted me to notice.

I got up and went back into the kitchen. When I again felt the wall of warmth and wondered aloud what I was supposed to see, my attention turned to the counter right behind the warm place. There was my empty crockpot, with no crock in it, still plugged in from the night before! I had left it on all night!

Do I believe an Angel came to me, to point this out to me for my safety? Yes, I do and am very grateful for the help.

They do not do this for only a select few, but for all of us. There was a time I believed that angels only answered the call of special people, or people with a grand life purpose. I guessed if you weren't Moses, or Noah, you weren't on their radar.

This belief may have come from being misinformed by well-intentioned people. When I was much younger, I was a member of a church that espoused the belief that there were no longer any miraculous manifestations of the Spirit. This included angelic intervention.

I now know that is not the case. They are here to protect all of us, and they are here to help us. The promise of angelic help is as true today as it was in biblical times.

Even though in this instance, I did not ask for help it was given. But I now believe that our angels can be even more effective in our lives if we will only ask.

Chapter 17

In the arms of angels

Josée Leduc

As a child, I always believed that I was special, that I could make a difference, and that I could help others. Deep down inside of me, I've always known that helping people in some way was my destiny. I'll never forget that day when it all began. It was on a beautiful sunny winter day. I was ten year solds and in grade four. I remember this like it was yesterday. The teacher had decided to let me leave earlier for being on my best behavior. *"Josée Leduc, you can leave; you've been good today,"* she said hoping that the other kids would listen and do the same in the future. So I got up from my desk and left the class. I went to my locker and got dressed in my snow suit. After putting on my winter boots, my mittens, and my winter hat, I came down the stairs and opened the school front doors to go outside. The sun was really bright as the rays were shining down on me.

I was so happy that I was leaving earlier that I didn't pay attention to my surroundings. So I didn't notice that there wasn't a volunteer helping the kids cross the road as usual. When I saw my mother and her friend waiting for me in the car on the other side of the street, I started running towards them unaware. Suddenly, I felt myself floating in the air. I remember having a sense that someone was looking down and smiling at me, having a beautiful light glow around him. What was odd is that I didn't feel any pain. Instead, I felt very comfortable like there was a warm breeze surrounding my little body. It was as if I was not in my body anymore, but rather, floating and watching myself from higher plane of existence. I wasn't scared or anything. In fact, I felt totally loved. Like a scene in a movie, I remember watching my mother getting out of the car, rushing towards me and screaming hysterically as she just realized what had just happened. As she was running towards my body, she was screaming to call the ambulance. Everyone in the school had heard the screaming and where watching from the windows. *"Oh look, I lost one of my boots,"* I thought to myself. *"Was I dead? Was I going to a better place?"* I questioned. No answers. Nothing. Only silence. Then, I heard a soft voice. *"Everything will be fine and you will be returning to your body very soon,"* it said gently. Apparently, I just had been run over by an oncoming car. What are the odds that a car was passing in front of the school exactly at the moment I was crossing the street?

A few moments later when I came to, I was lying on the ground. As my spirit was fully coming back to my body, I slowly opened my eyes. It was like waking up from a dream. I wasn't sure if it was real or not, but I was seeing various shapes and colors floating in the air and all around me. I rubbed my eyes to make sure I still wasn't dreaming and that I was seeing clearly. As I was still looking up, I saw my Angel standing there above me smiling. Slowly he drifted away as he was saying goodbye with a waving hand gesture. *"Angel! Angel mommy,"* I said softly as I reached my right hand up to the sky. My mother was lying next to me and didn't pay attention to what I was saying, because she was in total shock. The only thing that she could see was blood coming out on the side of my mouth and thinking OMG this isn't happening. *"Be okay! Be okay!"* cried my mother. As I was refocusing my attention to my mother, I could hear her saying with a trembling voice, *"Mommy loves you! Mommy loves you!"*

Once the police and ambulance came, there were more and more people around me. But something was different. At first, I couldn't put my finger on it, but somehow there was something different about the people surrounding me. It was like I could see different colors all around them just like the colors of the rainbow after the rain. What I didn't know back then is that I was seeing their life energy called aura. I didn't want to freak people out so I decided not to tell anyone, even my mother. I could see that she was still in shock from the accident and wouldn't understand what I was seeing. She had enough for one day. But I found it amazing that I could see what I could see even if I didn't fully understand what it meant and how it would help me later in life. Riding in the ambulance on my way to the hospital, I tried not to look directly at people, because I didn't want them to notice that I could see much more things with my eyes than normal people could. Seeing what I was seeing was going to change my perspective on everything and even on life itself, I told myself.

As soon as we got to the hospital, I was admitted and was brought into a room so that the doctor could examine me. I was no longer wearing my snow suit. They made me change into the blue linen shirt and made me lie down on the examination bed. Waiting for the doctor seemed like an eternity as my mother was getting impatient. But a several minutes later, the doctor opened the room door and said, "Hi! My name is Dr. Smith." He turned to look at me and said, *"So I hear that you were hit by a car,"* as he started examining me. My mother's hands were still trembling as she tried to explain to the doctor what had happened. After examining me, the doctor couldn't believe that I had nothing broken, no bruises and only a small scratch on the left side of my face. *"The accident should have killed you,"* he said to me. *"You are a very lucky little girl,"* concluded the doctor.

He turned to my mother and told her that if I felt fine, I could go back to school in a couple of days. Of course, he thought that the snow suit must have protected me from the impact and had probably saved my life. Doctors usually don't believe in miracles. For me, it could only be a miracle. And that's when my awakening began.

When I woke up the next morning, I was filled with a new sense of hope, encouragement, and vitality. My mother who slept with me that night had cooked my favorite breakfast, which was a slice of toast with cream cheese and a cup of hot chocolate with small delicious marshmallows in it. When I came back to school a few days later, all my friends came to see me in the school yard. They were all curious to find out how I was doing. *"Did it hurt?"* one said. *"Were you scared?"* the other said. I explained that I didn't see it coming and that I didn't feel anything when the car hit me. I wanted to tell them more, but I decided that the only important thing they really needed to know is that angels exist. *"Only my guardian angel could have saved me from that horrific accident that day and everyone has one,"* I later told them. From that moment on I started believing in miracles, believing in angels, believing in a higher plane of existence, and believing that life is much more than just a series of random coincidences. I am convinced that someone protected me that day and that this was my first encounter with my wonderful angel. Today, I have faith that they are always around me, that they are always listening if I need them, and that I'm never alone.

Although I have other unbelievable stories as this one while growing up, I've decided to share this particular one with you, because this is when it all began for me. I keep that early childhood event not only as a reminder, but also as a pleasant memory that this was the day that I really started to believe in life. Life is a journey full of stories and I believe that everyone has at least one great story to share. Today, I live my life to the fullest, because I think that life is really amazing and precious. My hope is that by reading this story, you will decide to live your life to the best of your abilities knowing that you are not alone so that you can create and write your own wonderful stories and take your destiny into your own hands.

Angel Kiss

Angel messages in my dreams

Deb Bergersen

Years ago, when my children were small, I had a dream that has stuck with me through the years. I have asked myself what would have happened had I not heeded the dream. My son was only about four or five at the time and starting kindergarten. The dream was so vivid, I woke up screaming *No!* It was so real that it proved difficult to pull myself out of it. I then realized my husband had been shaking me, trying to wake me up.

Prophetic dreams are not new to me. I have had many. As the details of the dream came back to me, I knew that it was a message from my Heavenly Team. It was a warning! The details of the dream were so vivid. As it involved my son, I knew how to change the outcome should it happen in real life.

They showed me a scene where my son was underwater, lifeless, in a bathtub at my mother's home. I tried to revive him, screaming for help. I poured out the details of the dream to my husband, voicing: *"Mom isn't there anymore. Why would we be at her house? We don't even live near there now. This can't happen! We waited so long for him to join our lives."* He tried to comfort me, finally convincing me to try to sleep again.

Several weeks later, my answers started showing up. The first sign was that we were returning home. We were going across country to visit a city north of where my mom had lived, where we would be stopping to visit with relatives. Memories of the dream came flooding into my mind. Details of what I had seen haunted my thoughts as we prepared to take our journey. I made preparations by checking to make sure none of the same clothing my son was wearing in the dream went with us. Checking the clothing he had laid out to take, sure enough, the very shirt he was wearing in the dream was in the pile of clothes. Quickly removing it from the stack, I tucked it into one of his drawers.

A sister-in-law was living in my mom's home at the time so we arranged a different place to meet with her and her children. We stayed in a hotel nearby with an indoor pool so that the kids would have something to do. Alternatively, we met with my husband's family at the hotel to avoid returning to my mother's home.

After spending a couple of days in the area, I let out a huge sigh of relief. We escaped the events I had dreamed about! I was so grateful that my beautiful young son had been safe in my care.

Once again, my prayers of gratitude poured out to my Heavenly Team!

CHAPTER 18

ANGEL PROTECTION

Kimla Dodds

"Don't make any hasty decisions now Mom. You are vulnerable and Dad just passed away."

"I know my sweet daughter, but I have the feeling a huge storm is coming and I do not have the funds to repair this family cottage if that happens. The real estate market is strong now in Jersey. I will get a good price especially if I sell it furnished. Anyways, every time I walk in, I keep seeing Dad sitting in his favorite chair telling me to make a new life for myself."

On September 21, 2011 I signed the closing papers on our family vacation cottage at the Jersey Shore. It had been our summer memory maker for twenty-three years. Mixed emotions ran through my entire energy field, but somehow I instinctively knew it was the right thing to do.

My good friend called from Phoenix, Arizona offering her beach house to me for the winter rental season. It was larger than mine, furnished, two streets away and four doors down from the ocean. What a wonderful offer! Where would I be without my friends in my life? They are always by my side whenever I need them the most. I accepted and asked if one of my colleagues could rent along with me. We were both alone and could use the company during the cold New Jersey winter ahead. It seemed like a win-win situation for my friend so she was very pleased at the arrangement.

Our morning coffee time is what I will always cherish. Ready to greet the day with the smell of hazelnut coffee brewing, hair in ponytails and comfy sweats, we made our intentions and drew an oracle card from our angel deck. Then checking our email, we made plans for the day. This one cool and crisp October morning I read my email out loud. Could this be real? It was an invitation to attend a certification seminar on Mediumship with my good friend from the U.K. The location of the seminar was to be in the south of France in the beautiful town of Reuilly. My eyes became larger when I read our accommodation was to be in a French Chateau called St. Michel.

"Wow, this is a gift of a lifetime!" I shouted.

Immediately, I had to pack as the plane was departing the next day from Newark, NJ to Paris, France. My roomie helped me to get my things together, placed my dear dog in a puppy palace, and offered to take me to the airport. In the background during all of this excitement was the loud beeping of a weather warning coming across the TV. It seems as though the perfect collision of two mighty storms were fast approaching. Then I heard the name, Hurricane Sandy. That got my attention.

"Roomie, what did he just say? Did I hear evacuation of the island?"

We ran outside, hurriedly brought in all of the patio furniture, cleaned out the fridge, turned off the water and closed all of the windows. No time to spare, we couldn't board the doors or the windows.

I felt badly leaving my roomie but she spoke with her elderly mother and decided to drive inland and ride out the storm with her. We held hands and prayed to the Archangels Michael, Gabriel, Raphael, and Uriel. Placing them in each corner of the property, we asked that they protect the house and calm the approaching storm. We quickly hugged each other, looked at our watches and climbed into her car leaving mine in the driveway. I took a deep breath and hoped for the best.

The traffic to the airport was heavy, but we arrived just in time. Boarding the plane to Paris, my heart was torn from leaving an intense weather situation to envisioning the most enthralling spiritual vacation I could ever dream of experiencing. Phoning my daughter and family as I was fastening my safety belt, I so wanted to hear their voices and tell them how much I loved them. They were very calm, suggesting that it would be a bad storm but the media was exaggerating the outcome.

"Nothing to worry about," they said. *"We've been through these hurricane alerts before. You go and enjoy yourself. You deserve it! "*

However they did begin to pack and plan to drive to friends that were located inland if things got to that point.

"Okay, but promise me you won't wait till the last minute, I pleaded."

Landing in Paris was a surreal happening. I do not speak French, so I had to pull up my big girl panties, claim my bag, and get to the train station as fast as I could. Thank the angels it went smoothly. I was so happy and relieved to greet my friend from the U.K. as we boarded the train to Reuilly and the Chateau.

Compiled by Jewels Rafter

Photos could not even begin to capture the essence of this magical castle called a Chateau. There was a chapel close to the main quarters filled with stained glass window art of Archangel Michael and Mother Mary. Gold embossed alters glistened, small ancient pews stood firm, and the smell of answered prayers hung in the air. I knelt down and quietly asked for the safety of my family, friends, and the island itself. A strong wind came up just then and closed the entrance door shut as if to say my prayers had been heard.

The seminar was led by a beautiful blond-haired man whose soul beamed white light. He welcomed me with open arms. We settled into our group and began to introduce ourselves. Quickly we bonded, unpacked, and prepared for lunch. Heading to the dining room, I took in the light and airy décor around me. The conversation was what I remembered. I was so excited to make new friends from around the globe.

The next day I was greeted by a sharp-witted and talented lad from Sweden. He knocked on my door so I could awaken and witness the sunrise over the rolling hills and countryside so famous for producing award-winning French wines. He seemed genderless and beamed his uniqueness with compassion and care. I struggled to sit by him in the class room area but so did everyone as we all felt his boundless energy. It was a day packed with meditations, tools of mediumship, and creating the groups synergy. By the end of the day, my inside clock was getting the best of me so I retired early giving thanks for an incredible opportunity I was living.

Day three began with our group in a moment of gathering. A rather serious tone came over us like a hush. I had not been updated on the storm as my phone and internet did not work in the Chateau. Our facilitator asked for a placement of intention. He then told us that the hurricane in New York and New Jersey was worse than anyone predicted. All communication, travel, and updates were at a standstill. He then introduced me by name. He asked for the group to place an intention by calling in the angels to protect my home, family, and friends from greater damage. Through a visualization and prayer he allowed each person to connect with my rental home and surround it with white light. The room was quiet I could hear the group breathing in and out. Afterwards, each student came up to me to describe the house exactly. They knew the color of the paint, and trim. They saw the white fence and the driveway made of sand. I was completely overwhelmed with emotion. Scared, amazed, and needing to keep my faith I went to my room instead of attending lunch with the others. I prayed, cried, and could only put this in the hands of the Lord.

It was a fascinating but very long week of me putting on a brave face. I was exhausted trying to get any bits and pieces of information from the States on "Hurricane Sandy." Saying goodbye to these incredible connected souls is something we all acknowledged could never happen. Our bonds were put into place so strongly that they will stand the test of time. No final "Goodbyes," only "Till we meet again."

My roomie was there to gather me from the airport and the stories were endless. My family was safe but had no power so they could not return to their bayside home. My dog was safe and so happy to see me. We were graciously welcomed to stay at my roomie's mother's home on the mainland as our beloved island was devastated. All bridges had been wiped out and the National Guard was called to action.

It was six weeks later that we finally had a makeshift bridge we could cross over the bay to check on our island homes. We arrived in a yellow school bus as a designated group. The island looked as if a world war had taken place. Military guards were everywhere. Camouflaged Jeeps flew by kicking up incomprehensible amounts of sand. Cars were being extracted from the bay. There were bits and pieces of homes, rooftops, and unidentified objects strewn about thoughtlessly. Wires were not to been seen. The smell of gas brought tears to our eyes. My roomie and I were under strict rules to only bring one suitcase on the bus to place our most important items in. Holding hands, hearts pumping, we came down to our street. It was a mass of sand and destruction. Homes had been randomly extracted from the coastline and neighborhood streets. It looked like a mouthful of missing teeth.

Then there is was. Our rental home was perfect and standing bravely waiting for its medal of honor. Much to my surprise my car was parked in the driveway just like we left it. I was amazed it started right up! We watched as our neighbors had to locate a shovel to dig in just to get to their front doors only to be greeted by a wall of four feet of water inside. Believe me, there was not a spec of sand, water, damage or displacement to anything in or around our home. It was the only home that still had the fencing in place. We opened the back sliding doors and after six weeks, the fruit in the bowl we left on the kitchen counter was fresh and had shown no signs of spoilage whatsoever. The flowers I left on my desk still had water and were standing at attention.

We cried and got down on our knees, so grateful that our home was protected. However, the compassion and sadness we felt for everyone else was simply gut-wrenching. We boarded the school bus again to return to the mainland as our two hours were up. The crying and sobbing I will never forget. Some of our neighbors had nothing to place in their suitcases.

Their homes were not even there, everything completely gone. It was, again, one of those times when I experienced the happiness of knowing how powerful the angels are and then feeling the souls of despair that lost everything they worked so hard for in their lives.

My roomie and I talked about this real experience many times on our radio shows. Validating the greatness of the angels and how they will always come to your aide to protect and guide you. It is with a heavy heart I disclose my roomie lost her battle to breast cancer and is now flying high among the angels watching out for me as well. This chapter is dedicated to her and her never-ending belief in the power of angels.

May the angels protect and guide you and yours. Reach out! They are waiting to hear from you.

God Bless.

Kimla Dodds

Compiled by Jewels Rafter

SECTION 5
CHANNELED MESSAGES

SECTION 5

CHANNELED MESSAGES

Jewels Rafter

Attempts by Angelic and Spirit Guides to channel information to us are not at all rare, but actually quite frequent. Channeling happens in various ways, from focusing energy to affect thoughts, feelings, or even physical objects, to assuming the use of someone's hand, mind, or vocal cords to channel messages in a more direct manner.

Guidance for all on the earth plane flows steadily from the spirit world, and those with spiritual awareness know this from firsthand experience. Even those who are less aware have had sudden insight or inspiration that seems to come from "out of the blue." Our Guides, Angels, and loved ones in the spirit world can focus spiritual energy and direct it to subtly influence our thoughts, feelings, and behaviors, or to get specific messages through to us.

All earthly occupations are served by the Angelic and Spirit world. Master guides and teachers continually move between heaven and earth, channeling their energies to bring information through for our own and the planet's benefit. For example, in the world of science, ideas are given through inspiration, insight, or subtle influencing of thoughts about how to solve a particular problem or create a new invention or technology.

Invisible hands of light guide the hands of those in the medical field, helping to achieve a positive outcome for patients. A child may display unusual artistic or musical talent, influenced by a spiritual master in that field. A teacher's words may elevate the thoughts and feelings of those listening, and the unscripted words flow so fluently that even the teacher's words seem to flow out of nowhere. In all of these cases, the energies of the Angels or celestial beings and the earthly person flow together for the purpose of achieving the best result.

It is time for humans to be aware that love can and does pass from these other realms down to us who now inhabit this earth plane. It's true that there are countless beings who watch over us and send love, although not everyone has been unreserved to receiving it. Now, however with the spiritual awakening and the thinning of the veil, telepathic communication between spirit and the earth plane has hugely increased. More and more humans are becoming aware of the guidance and love that is available from the spirit world. Once we begin to accept this love and guidance, we can know security, peace, bliss, and perhaps for the first time in centuries, we can communicate with the other celestial dimensions openly.

Not only is love passing from other realms to earth, but so is help and guidance. We need only to ask with sincerity and patience, and we will receive guidance. Guidance will come in many forms. Most people will receive it in the form that is most comfortable and most compatible with their natures. Some may receive help in dreams; some may receive pictures or visions; still others may hear spoken guidance. No matter how we receive this information, it is all conveyed to us telepathically. There are those in nearby realms whose joyful duty is to help us here on earth with this transition. These Spirit Guides are ready to send us all the information we require. We only need to clear ourselves and open up to receiving it.

The new ray of energy flooding the planet is increasing the rate of the vibration on earth and with it our personal vibratory rates. New telepathic centers in our bodies are being activated allowing us to pursue new avenues of communication. Telepathy and channeled messaging are some of these avenues which may be the most useful to us at this point in time. Our Angels and Spirit Guides are detached from our earthly problems, yet they still love us and wish to help guide us. During any situation or challenge, we can turn to them for assistance unconditionally. Our task is to open ourselves up so that we are receptive to their guidance and then adjust our lives in accordance with it.

It is inevitable; our lives will change once we open ourselves to their guidance. We might as well tune into the new energy and make changes as joyful and uplifting as possible. By opening up to the opportunity to connect, we allow messages of hope and peace to come through and uplift us.

There are many ways of channeling messages from our Angels. The easiest way is to sit quietly with a pen and paper or at your laptop and meditate quietly for a moment. Clear your mind of any prior thoughts or emotions from your day, and concentrate on your breathing. Let it become the only aspect you are focusing on. Breathe deeply and slowly and then ask either aloud or in your mind, a question.

This may be question such as:

- What am I supposed to be learning from "this specific situation"?

- What should I be focusing on to move forward?
- What elements am I missing or omitting to see?
- What is in my best interest to know at this very moment?
- What can you tell me that would be of benefit to my challenges right now?

Type your question and just see what comes out when you put your fingers on the keys. Just start writing about anything that comes into your head, just as you would if you were journaling about your day. The trick with this is to get used to going with the flow and not question the information that is flooding in. The more you're used to writing, the easier it is to get into that "flow" state when writing, where you can channel your inner sage.

In my experience, channeled information tends to be high vibrational in nature. It will often comfort you, provide clarity or will raise your mood in some way. If it feels negative or feels heavy, you're probably not channeling a source that you want to tap into or you may just be channeling your own emotional body, if you are not feeling very good or feeling unsure or insecure.

So how do you know if you're really speaking to a spirit and not just yourself? Initially you won't know. Doing this kind of work requires opening yourself up and trusting. My advice is to just keep writing, keep going. Don't filter or evaluate your conversation until the very end. If you filter what you're hearing you're going to block the connection. Thinking thoughts like, *"I wonder if this is just me talking to me,"* will knock you out of state. The longer you go, the stronger the connection will get.

Let the session come to a natural close, thank the Angel of Guide for speaking to you, and close down your connection by drawing your energy back close to your body. The more often you do this, the more likely you'll be able to tell when it's just you talking to you and when you are communicating with spirit. When you're in contact with the other dimension, they will tell you things that you would not necessarily say to yourself. It can take a few sessions to get it right so don't give up.

Angel kiss

Angel's kiss

Jennifer Del Villar

How can one so utterly beautiful and shiny ever become that which self-cages itself in a cocoon of unworthiness? It's quite easy actually. As we allow ourselves to be guided by a sense of shame, guilt, and being less than – it's easy to paint ourselves into the corner of our hearts. We let fear and self-negativity tell us that we are not the elegant and radiating crystal souls that we truly are. That those around us who seem to have glorious and noble existences appear to be the chosen ones. But when we step back and allow our inner guides, our inner voices, our inner angelic beings to speak truthfully in a state of peace and love, we can realize that we are all one and we are all worthy.

The journey of self, the journey of now, the journey of one is a majestic tapestry that connects all of our puzzle pieces together. We are never alone, truly; but we are all unique and necessary in our own lightness. Never unworthy, never discounted, never abandoned – only love. Sit in the quiet and know thyself. Sit in the splendor of the beings that surround you; and let them sing to you the song of love. Open the gift of your soul and celebrate you.

Oh child, as I call forth into the beating of your heart, hear these words:

> *How can it be that your light has dimmed?*
>
> *How can it be that your words have tarnished?*
>
> *How can it be that your vision became cloudy?*
>
> *How can it be that your smile has diminished?*
>
> *Come now find the brightness within you.*
>
> *Come now speak the syllables dipped in silver.*
>
> *Come now vision self-infused in radiance.*
>
> *Come now frown dissipate into gladness.*

In the hopefulness of each and every day I say this unto you. You, yes you, ride on the wings of angels and glorious beings of light. You are that glorious being of light. You are the mist in the morning, you are the rain that feeds the gentle earth and becomes the fertility of new life. You are the effervescence of the dancing seeds of the dandelion that fly through the air. You are the wind that carries the seeds across the plains. You are the fire that ignites within the volcano and spews forth that which creates islands. You are the memory of all that is, the now experience and the hope of all to come. Never doubt, never cage that which is a giver of life and light to this glorious sphere that is never ending and always beginning. You are glorious – radiate and think upon that beautiful soul.

Chapter 19

Love is always the answer

Barbara Grace Reynolds

Fourteen years ago, I was in a sixteen-year marriage where I had always worked extremely hard to make things perfect for everyone else. I was the perfect wife, the perfect employee, the perfect everything. I woke up one day and I realized that I was not happy and I just couldn't pretend any more. After many tears, I came to the realization that things would have to change. I gave my ex the option of changing with me or leaving. You can tell by my calling him my ex which choice he made. So I began a journey of "fixing" me. I had read lots of metaphysical books and I had even been trained as a Coach so I knew that I could "fix" me. After several months of using logic to correct my life, since that was the logical thing to do, I accepted that I didn't know the answers so I finally asked for guidance (asking is the secret to receiving). I was guided to a process called automatic writing.

Automatic writing seemed simple enough. Get your pen and paper then you begin by repeating this statement three times: *"I am now receiving what is for my highest good from the highest possible source,"* and then write down your question and wait for the answer to flow. I have seen lots of people attempt this process and I figured it would take a while to get an answer, and I was determined to be patient. I said the statement three times, wrote my question, and my hand started writing so fast that I had to yell, *"Slow down!"* Yes, my Angelic guidance was that eager to work with me. Of course my wonderful logical mind said, *"I'm making this up,"* but my heart felt different. And when I read what I had written, it was definitely not my style of writing at all. It seemed more old world style of writing and there were lots of "we" and "us", and no "I" or "me."

Everything that happens in our lives allows us to develop skills and strength. This was my journey to learn Trust and Love. I began asking question after question. I wanted to understand everything that had ever happen in my life. Some of the answers that I received just did not make any sense to me, at that time. I realize now that my whole mindset was being changed but at that time I was just frustrated. But I continued to ask, and ask, and ask. One day I realized that I was not just writing the answers, I was also hearing them. That gave me even more freedom to ask. I could be driving along in my car just carrying on a conversation with my Guides. Some people probably wondered about my sanity, but I did not let anyone's opinions stop me. This was my way to finally gain some understanding about life, about who I was, about why things were as they were.

As time went on I began to notice that my Angels would often answer my questions with just one word, "LOVE", which made no sense at all to me, so I would challenge their answer. I would accuse them of trying to avoid giving me a real answer. It finally got to the point where they began to say, *"That is the answer. Even if you don't yet understand why, it does not change the answer. You can accept it or not. We will continue to Love you no matter what. It is your choice."* And that really ticked me off! How can you have an argument with that kind of an answer? So I changed tactics and I really started to listen. I asked to be shown the Truth. I asked to be allowed to see. I began to Trust.

And now I am ready to share what I have learned after all these years of my conversations with all the wonderful Archangels, Angels, Goddess, Ascended Masters, and other Divine Beings that I have come to know as "My Team."

These Angelic beings taught me that we actually create everything that happens in our lives with what we believe. So our beliefs about Love have a huge impact on our lives. If we believe that love hurts, then we tend to push Love out of our lives to keep ourselves safe. This includes love of self. People who push Love away spend a lot of their time suffering and struggling. This is because Love energy is always flowing around and through each of us, so when we are pushing Love away, we are shutting down or excluding an important part of who we are.

Why do we fear Love? What we have been taught or programmed to believe about Love is not true. Many of us have never ever allowed ourselves to feel Pure Love. And no, Pure Love is not the stuff of romance novels. It is much, much deeper. Pure Love is the energy that flows from your heart, not your mind. Pure Love has no conditions, so you cannot earn it. Pure Love is a gift of God's energy to you.

We have heard about Pure Love and its unconditional state but we are also told that wars are fought over love and people fight other people for love. Fighting is never unconditional so it can never be Pure Love.

These divine beings told me that Pure Love is about freedom. Allowing yourself to accept yourself, exactly as you are. Now our minds fight against that kind of acceptance. If you are coming from Pure Love then it releases any need to judge, so what do you think about? Your mind is afraid that it will die if you live in Pure Love. After all, we have been taught for so many centuries that the mind is important, that intellect determines value, that the more initials you have after your name, the better a person you are. How can we ever survive without our minds creating problems and reasons for our very lives?

So this tells you that living from Pure Love requires a lot of changes to beliefs. It requires changes to your whole mindset. It requires that you recreate you, which definitely brings up fear in many people.

We are taught to base our identity on our beliefs. Now the ones who taught us this failed to mention that over 99% of what we believe is actually not true, which means that what we believe about ourselves is also not true. So we live our lives in false identities. Some people have so many identities that they have no idea of who they really are. Their identity changes depending on who they are with. And yet they wonder why they can never be happy.

The more identities you have created for yourself, the more you are hiding from yourself. You hide so that you do not have to feel. You hide so that no one can know you or blame you. You hide from the guilt and shame you have bestowed upon yourself. How can you Love and accept yourself when you refuse to see your True Self or allow your True Self to be seen?

Living in Pure Love requires strength and confidence. It requires Trust in Source. It requires a letting go of what has been so that you can see what is. Pure Love requires change and that change give you back your life. Pure Love is the vibrational frequency which Angels emanate from. It is a beautiful peaceful energy.

And all of this realization about Love has allowed me to see so much about my own life and what I have been creating. It has brought me an understanding of why, when I was working so hard to be a good person and take care of everyone else, I was never happy. I can see now how I did not love myself. I can see now that the person I was being was merely a tiny portion of the potential that is within me. I can see how I was living in fear and hiding my true self.

All of this realization has changed my life. I went from being the person who helped other people to see more in themselves to being a strong powerful woman who knows that she has value and deserves to create a wonderful life for herself. I have gone from trying to "fix" myself and others to coaching people to freedom and empowerment. I have gone from being stuck in old beliefs to using Infinity Healing to release false beliefs and stand in the Truth. I have gone from reading lots of books to find the answers to being a conscious channel and getting the answers directly. Thanks to my Angels and their divine guidance, I have come to love myself and trust in Pure Love. Now I am certain that Love truly is the answer.

Angel kiss

Land of angels
Erica Johansen

Looking for inspiration to let the creative juices flow, I turned on the music and ecstatically danced with heart and soul. I felt a story stir and took breaks to write this tale:

> *"In the Land of Angels, within our lands, are leather-bound golden scrolls. Words for angels who tend the people, the flowers, and grasses of Earth.*
>
> *Your flowers and grass were planted by creator. Delivered into your steed, your protective wings.*
>
> *Watch over thy seed. Frail yet tough, naïve and brilliant, fearful yet loving. Help it find its balance between the duality in its nature. Protect, as it grows.*
>
> *Talk sweetly to your flowers, your grasses. Giving comfort, encouragement and guidance. Be a messenger for creator and illuminate the way to grow... to grow.*
>
> *Thy grass may never know you are there. Fertilize with miracles. Watch over as twists and turns in the winds, dancing for father sky. Seed's intention reaches for sun, rain, and growth.*
>
> *Thy flower may shrink next to the beauty of another. Teach that they may grow together in the same light. Watch its lushness as it peaks, the flower unfurls into the sun.*
>
> *For you are the Angels of my masterpiece garden to be called upon. When thy flower calls your name, answer."*

I thought to myself, this is too "fairy tale" and tossed it aside. I then heard, "Your story hasn't finished itself. Go to the bookstore for inspiration tomorrow."

In the morning I walked into the bookstore with purpose. I went to where I thought the Angel section was and froze. It was the book I wished for: and I snatched it up! Not finding the Angel section, I sat hoping for inspiration from the book I was holding. An Angel section was the last chapter of the book and popped open to the first page. Within a minute of reading… chills. The mention of the sacred text, The Talmud. *"Every blade of grass has its own angel that bends over and whispers grow, grow."*

That line matched my fairy-tale I wrote, coincidence? Hmm. I bought the book and left.

Back at home the story wrote itself. The voice of the author narrated in my head and my fingers typed to keep up! The words "Let's Fly" unfurled onto the pages. I heard, *"Your story isn't finished. Go visit your friend for the ending."* I didn't understand but I swung by Bestie's house. My mind wondered to the Talmud, I knew nothing about, so I looked it up on-line. Chills again, as I read about the golden-hued Scrolls of the Talmud, the shas, the six orders.

Now I don't know which part of this is divine communication or channeled messages but I'll take it as an Angel's kiss. One thing I do know, is that my Guardian Angels are there guiding me every step of the way. Amen

Angel kiss

Merge with the angels' meditation
Wendy James

This is a reading meditation.

Allow yourself the gift of relaxing into it with perfect love and perfect trust.

Shh...Do you hear the wings?

This is your sacred moment.

Allow relaxation to seduce you.

Feel tension melt away willingly.

Peace is yours to have.

Let these words breathe into you,

> *"I am not alone.*
>
> *I am not alone.*
>
> *I am not alone."*

Open up further and hand away all hesitation.

Your wings are rising slowly for a well needed stretch.

Can you see them in your heart's eye?

So strong.

So beautiful.

What color are they at this moment?

You feel stillness move through you. Your feathered extensions absorb harmony's sound.

Give way to all your senses, including those majestic wings.

Let them stretch, flex and ease.

Your soul wants to fly and these wings will carry you.

Bring your thoughts into your heart.

Where does it want to fly to?

Let these words breathe into you,

> "I am limitless and free.
>
> I am limitless and free.
>
> I am limitless and free."

You soar, flying freely carried by your perfect wings. From above you can see the journey.

Winged eyes see from hearts pure view.

Swoop and spin like an eagle. Flutter like a humming bird. Maneuver like an owl.

Feel the rush of life as you blow through it. It's exhilarating!

Your vision is acute. All things can be seen. Is there a place you see to land?

Allow yourself to explore. In this place you will find what you seek. It's just there, in front of you.

Observe it with no expectations or attachments. This is what your heart brought you to see.

How lucky are you to be able to trust yourself this way!

Let these words breathe into you,

> "I am healthy, whole and complete.
>
> I am healthy whole and complete.
>
> I am healthy whole and compete."

You are an angel. Follow your heart and it will lead you to contentment.

Let your wings bring you to those you can help. Help abundantly because you can.

Let your wings comfort you when you are lost.

You are a piece of all that is. Give back to the world out of love for yourself.

Remember to stretch your wings and let your heart carry you forward.

Remember that you are here with great purpose.

Remember that relaxation and harmony are found by going within.

Meditation can quickly bring you to the sacred and limitless self where anything is possible.

Practice playing within this soul space.

Your own inner angel waits to fly with you again.

Chapter 20

Message from the Angels

Tracie Mahan

I am excited to be here as part of this amazing book. The question put to me for this book was "How am I inspired by Angels?" I would say that I have always known I had Angels with me. I grew up Catholic and learned about Angels and Archangels during my adolescence. It wasn't until I was in my late teens or early 20's that I really understood how powerful they could be in my life. I knew they were there, and that they would help if I ever was in a life-threatening situation, but I did not understand fully how helpful they could be in my day to day life.

I learned a lot about prayer from my Mother as I grew up. She was very inspirational with her prayers and teaching me the importance of them. However, even she hadn't been fully informed, through the Catholic teachings, as to how to bring our Angels in closer. As we both learned together, about free will and non-interference, we began to understand their restrictions and learning how to work with the Angels. They need our invitation for them to guide us and inspire us more fully. They are not to interfere with us as a rule, unless we have asked them to help us in our day or we are faced with a life-threatening experience before our time to go.

So with this information I started to say a prayer that went like this: *"God, please send me Angels to surround me, guide me, and protect me."* This prayer sent me on a journey of synchronistic events that changes the way I look at the world I live in.

It has been years now that I have consciously communicated with my Angels. I suppose I have always interacted with them, even as a small child.

In my 20's I started to notice I would get psychic impressions, knowings, and an understanding of people beyond the surface of what they were showing visibly. This is when I started to learn more about my Angels, through synchronicity, through classes, and through seeking, and oh-boy what a journey that has been.

People often ask me, *"How do you connect with your Angels?"* This question really made me sit back and look at what it truly is that I do to connect, hear, and ultimately understand what they are telling me. I find that when

I connect with my Angels, or anyone else's Angels for that matter, what I am doing is I become a blank slate in my mind, and I allow the Angels to use my thoughts to communicate with me. The impressions that come in are indeed much different than the way I would think, talk, or express myself. It is in recognizing that expression that I realized this is my Angels speaking. This is also how I got started in doing Channeled letters from the Angels and working with giving people messages from their Angels.

So for this chapter in the book, what I thought I would do is channel a letter. Here is a channeled letter from the Angels to you, the Readers of this book.

> *Channel:*
>
> *Hello beloveds. We are excited to have this opportunity to share with you and communicate with you in such a way. There are many who are seeking more truth in the world at this time. You are a seeker of truths. That is why you are reading this now. You are either starting your awakening process or you are well on your way; either way, you are opening up to what life on Earth is truly about. As you find yourself getting more and more connected to the source of who you really are, you will expand your own gifts in this world exponentially. There is so much to take in and so much love and beauty to grab hold of. We say to you, that it is time to put the pettiness behind you and move into a great new future for yourself, and for those you love.*
>
> *We have observed you for many lifetimes. We have watched your evolution over these lifetimes and in the many challenges you have taken on. It is in this time of your incarnation that you will see more truth and remember more of who you truly are, than ever before. The human form is a glorious gift to have. So many have forgotten what a true gift it is to have the human experience. If it were not for the human experience, we would not be able to evolve as a whole in all that is. It is in experiencing the emotional fluctuations that you learn and evolve. As you learn and evolve you bring each of those experiences back with you to the collective body. As a collective we all take from your experiences and learn from your emotions.*
>
> *There are many planets and life forms to choose from, but none are like this one. It takes many rotations through this form to really gather it all in. To experience all of life in all its forms.*
>
> *There are some souls that have never had this experience and truly honor the strength and courage it takes to come into the Earth realm. The ones*

who have come into this world came in to take on the challenges of forgetting who they truly are, to work with free will, and have little information about their true being, and with all of that going on, then to see if they could navigate their way home again. It is a magical journey, but most will only get how magical when it is their time to leave the journey and remember why they were there in the first place. As your world often says, it is in the "hindsight" that you see the truth in it all.

So we ask of you, please enjoy your journey. Love from your purest of hearts, and be true to your authentic self. Let go of the illusion that you must FOLLOW. Be the leader in changing the world into the divine experience it was always intended to be. See the magic in all life. Spend time daily connecting with your divine beings that are with you always. Call in your Angels to guide you through each day and be open to the guidance you are given.

Life, as we see it from here, is a true gift of connection. You experience love on so many levels there. Don't waste your time trying to be right, or rich, or powerful. Just be authentic and true and loving to yourself and others, then you will see what we mean by magical. So many get lost in the pursuit to be something greater and creating a legacy. These can be fun accomplishments along your journey, but do not get lost in them. It is when you get lost in the world created by man, that you get lost in your purpose for being here. This is why it is so important to make the most of your connections with the desire to seek the truth.

So many illusions have been taught to your conscious mind, that it is hard to know which way is up and which way is down. As we all form a collective in love, we will defeat the no longer needed illusion that there is not enough. Your world will change in ways you cannot even imagine, and you will co-create your life in ways you have always dreamed of. We are most pleased that you are on this leg of the journey with us. We applaud your courage, wisdom, and strength as you move forward with your purpose in life. May you always feel the connection and know your way.

Thank you for your most blessed time today in reading this message. Call on us always and often, we are here to help you move through your life maze with ease and grace while here on the Earth Realm.

With great love and gratitude.

The Angels.

So in the creating of this letter above, what I had done was ask the Angels what it is they would like to say? Then I cleared my mind and began to write the thoughts that were coming through. I find this process to be full of love and incredibly insightful. Not only do I feel blessed to bring the messages in, but I also can feel the energy of the divine messengers as they are bringing the messages into my thoughts.

I encourage you to try this; say a prayer and call in your Angels close to you. Ask them a question and then put the thoughts that are coming in onto paper or type them out. It is a wonderful experience. I will say that it takes some practice though, so please give this a couple of tries. Keep in mind this may not be the tool for you to communicate with your Angels, so if you do find this method hard to do, please try other ways to connect. I promise you it is worth it.

Many blessings to you on your journey, and may you see the magic along the way.

Chapter 21

Channeled Message Living the Halo Life

Brian D. Calhoun

Imagine living the life of an Angel here upon the earth, having more than enough of anything you could ever imagine in all areas of life. Imagine that this life of Heaven on Earth is now real and true.

We are here to let you know that this is very much the case. However, there is a part of you that doesn't believe that this is even possible and cannot imagine how one can amass such greatness. We, Angels, want you to know that as soon as you began to imagine a life of Heaven's Riches in Love, Light, Wealth, Health, or anything, that we began to help align you to the pathways to make it so.

You think that it is all airy fairy New Age stuff, but we are here to let you know that it is truth! We want you to believe in the possibility of living such a life and thus suspend your beliefs that it could never happen to you. You are worthy of such goodness but do not believe you are. Sure you think that you are worthy in many ways, but the problem is that your subconscious mind doesn't believe it is. If you did believe you were and believed in the power of who you are as a divine creator, you would already be living such an existence.

For the simple truth is, you are living the life you think deep down you are worthy of, and you are experiencing everything that you believe to be true. It doesn't matter if it is positive or negative. Energy goes where beliefs lay. Therefore, if you want to change your life, then it is time to change your thoughts! That is where it all begins.

You have heard this before, but the thing is dear one, you have only heard part of the message and you rejected the rest of it. You haven't truly felt the power of the energy of the words and therefore remain stuck in your life in some way. You want to rise above the current circumstances and have called up to us to help you many times in many ways. We have heard you time and again. Every time we answer your call. But you still hold yourself in place, stuck in a time loop where you keep repeating the same thoughts, words, and actions, over and over again.

We have sent you many a teacher to help you free yourself and help you shift on many levels, and to some you have listened and let them help you. For others, you have resisted what they have offered you and therefore rejected the divine assistance that we have sent to you. Lucky for you, we love you so and will continuously send you divine messages, help, and blessings in answer to your call.

You see, we perceive you as very intelligent beings who don't need our assistance in any way, for you are the source of it all, and thus as source, you have the power to create or recreate your life at all. We feel just blessed and lucky to be able to help such an important being on the earth level as you requested when you came into the world, decided to forget who you were in the bigger picture and decided to experience the not haves, in order to know what the haves are! You see, one cannot experience or know the other, without having experienced the other side of the equation first. You put into place triggers to help you shift and to help you remember and reconnect to the power of who you are along the pathways.

Some of these triggers aren't always so fun and light-filled. For these triggers may be soulmates that push your buttons or really get "under your skin." The greatest gift of these soulmates is the lessons and experiences that they help you experience, learn, and grow from. They are only answering your call to help you with this journey on the earth. They as divine beings of love, felt honored when you asked them to play the role of the "villain" in your story. They knew it wouldn't be easy to play the role and they would have to truly make you believe them. They knew that you would also be answering their calls and teaching them as well. You both loved each other enough that you also knew once you got through it, you could choose to forgive and move past the experience so that you could experience more loving experiences once again.

You knew that the experiences would play out in all areas of your life on the earth, whether it was in your relationships, finances, career, health, or an infinite number of other ways. You knew deep within that you would never be alone and that we would be here helping you through each moment of the journey, and that everything that was happening would be in the highest good of all concerned.

You knew that you would remember this divine truth at the perfect moment and that with the remembrance would come a peace from remembering that love was all that is real and true. Today, you are being granted another opportunity to shift and bring forth the light of your soul into the world as you know it and recreate that which appears before you.

You are being granted the knowledge that you are perfect, whole, and complete in all ways, and that there is nothing outside of yourself. All that appears is an illusion and thus not real. Think of it much like a movie;

you can change the movie playing out at any time by putting a new one in the player.

Sure, there is a part of you that has always known this truth, and that part of you is always living your heavenly life. It never has separated or feared. It has only loved and appreciated the totality of it all. It is consistently reminding you in your dream states, in your subconscious and conscious minds, and experiences of such divine high spiritual truths. It is always helping you to remember yourself as who you have always been.

You are the Divine! Whether you wish to call the wholeness of your Spirit, God, Universe, Light, Source, or any other word, it doesn't matter or diminish the fact that this remembrance is what can shift you and your world. It is not enough to know it and to experience it. You must become your true nature, your whole self, the *Divine*.

You must act as if you are God, in a loving state being and as only your soul knows itself to be, and thus reflect that into the world. By doing so, you will begin to shine light upon the darkness. Remember God is Love, so be Love in all experience and come from this place in all ways and times.

Know all as God appearing in human form and thus giving back to itself. Remember, everything is energy and that energy is within you, here and now.

To illustrate this further, we will let you know that you are having a divine communication with yourself here and now. You are the one that typed these words and created the book you are now reading from. You have created every aspect that is life. This divine energy has flowed through you from your soul into the invisible realm of the universes and then has come back to you, having taken shape and form as this experience, here and now.

This same analogy can be used in terms of Health, Abundance, Love or anything else. You are one with it all and it is all one with you. Remember to be this and you will experience your own personal miracles in quick manner.

So today, make the choice to let go what no longer serves you in beliefs, thoughts, words, or whatever else and let in the light of the divine replenish you and your life.

You think that money comes from your employer or client, or another source. But in truth money is nothing more than your own energy flowing to you through you. It is time to start changing the way you see everything and start remembering that all is one. It is through this remembrance that you will begin to live life fully once again.

Remembering who you are and stepping into your power will release you from the burdens that your life has become. Remembering that you are the source, the substance, and the energy of everything is empowering. It is when you feel empowered, that you will choose to experience love further. Remember, you are worthy of having very loving experiences, for Love is who you are and all that is.

This all is good news because it is showing you that you have the power to change anything, for you are the power that has created it all and we are with you supporting you all along the way.

Let us show you it in another way. Upon the time you were born, your cells were given enough breath to last a lifetime. You knew this to be true, had faith in the process, and just went about the task of growing up. You made the most of your childhood, your adolescence, early adulthood, and even to this very day with this continuous flow of breath. Yes, perhaps at times you had breathing problems and for some of you, still do. But you hope and trust that you will be able to take another breath somehow some way, and you don't even think about where it is coming from. You just know it is going to be there.

The same is true when it comes to many of the body's functions and energy systems. You just trust in the innate power within to take care of it all. When you get sick, you pray that you will be healed and for the most part you believe you will, and thus forth health is restored. When something isn't healed it is because there are some beliefs still in the way of the healing or a lesson in play. Once the lesson is learned and the beliefs released, then healing takes place. This can sometimes happen in an instant, and will be called a miracle.

The truth is when one is lacking anything, it is because there is a belief at play, and that has caused a disconnection of source energy within to take place. Once that has unfolded, the energy radiates into the world as a lack of. Good news is, everything can be made anew again and is done as soon as a shift takes place within the belief and you are reconnected to who you truly are.

It is our hope today that you will begin to see everything and yourself as you truly are - a continuous flowing energy that provides more than enough of everything in all experiences that may be required for the journey. So therefore, trust and have faith that whatever you give out, will expand and come through you back to you continuously.

You pay a bill and the funds that you utilized for that will be replenished just like the air you breathe out and in again. You share love in some way; love will expand and bless you again. You use energy for exercise or something in your life; it too will be refreshed and renewed. Everything will flow through you into the world and then come back to you in some way and time. If you will have faith and trust in the process you will be blessed.

All too often we see that you limit the way that things can unfold, when in truth there are an infinite number of ways that something can happen.

Think of it this way. You give a gift to someone on their birthday. You aren't giving it because you expect anything back from them, usually. You are giving freely from the place of love and joy. Your divine self knows that there is more good flowing and guides you so along the path to it. It doesn't have any attachments of when it may be returned or how or anything of such. It just freely shares of itself continuously. When one lets attachments and expectations go, miracles unfold and what was put out into the universal realms find their way back to the source, **You**, in wonderful ways.

Each day, make a point to take a moment to remind yourself who and what you are, and connect to the omnipresence of your true nature. This can be done in a variety of ways, including meditation on your heart and soul connection.

Take a moment right now to take a few deep breaths as you bring your awareness within, with your hands placed on your chest and on your stomach regions.

As you breathe in and out, become aware of your beating heart. Allow yourself to feel connected to all that is with each beat your heart takes. Do this for a couple minutes as you breathe deeply in and out. Keep your focus on your beating heart and breathing for the next few moments, before continuing onward.

Now, become aware of your hand on your stomach, or solar plexus as it is often called. Imagine a beautiful bright light deep within, much like the light of the sun. This is your soul light. See it expanding as you feel yourself transmuting every cell of your being with love, allowing it to radiate into the world at large to touch, awaken, and expand the light within all. Do this for the next few moments and then continue when ready.

As you feel your heart beating and your breath moving in and out, allow yourself to feel deep within your cells a continuous energy source flowing.

This energy is the source of all creation and is responsible for all of health, abundance, love, and the connecting energy of it all. Feel yourself bathing in this energy as it expands, radiates, and flows into the universe for all to enjoy.

Feel yourself connected to the heavens and to the earth, as you feel yourself connected to all that is, isn't, and all between, and know yourself one with all. Feel yourself in the ebb and flow of love, wealth, health, knowledge, and everything else you can imagine as you give your gratitude for everything, known and unknown, as the continuous divine energy flows freely through you, to you, by you.

Doing this exercise daily for a few moments will strengthen your connection to yourself, and help you live your halo life in totality as you begin to remember and experience who you are.

We wish to thank you for allowing us to guide, remind, and reconnect here all along the way.

As always with love,

Your Angels

ANGEL KISS

TRUST IS THE KEY
Barbara Grace Reynolds

Life often throws you curved balls but when you are tapped into your own GPS (Guidance Pivotal to Success) you are never lost. This is something that I have seen many times in my life. There was a time that I was going to see a friend who lives several miles from the nearest town in an area where the roads don't have names, they are just long numbers. I had been to her house once before but I didn't have a clear idea of exactly how to get there. It's a three-hour drive and I knew how to get to within thirty miles of her since it was interstate highways but what exit to take and where to go from there, I didn't know. So I started talking with my Guidance and really listening. They got me off the highway and onto some back road. I didn't recognize any landmarks or signs. I just did as I was guided to do. Needless to say I made it. I actually made it there faster than when I was riding with someone who knew how to get there. I found out later that she didn't tell people about the way that I came because most people got confused and lost when using that route. I guess they weren't using their GPS!

My Guidance used to have me just get in my car and drive. I never knew where I was going. I took the turns that I was guided to take, even though my brain was telling me to go a different way. I realize now that it was one of the ways they were building my trust in Guidance. Making that shift from thinking that your brain has all the solutions to your problems, especially after you have had so much education, to just trusting in your unseen Guidance can be a big thing. I did have members of my family who told me that I must be crazy to just go driving off alone, not knowing where I was going. They kept telling me all the bad things that could have happened. Which helped me to remember that nothing bad every happened on any of those drives. Trusting in my Guidance has even saved my life a few times.

Now I don't understand why anyone would want to have to figure things out on their own. It's like having a computer and never using the Internet. Why limit your own life? You have just as much access to Guidance as I do. Are you ready to connect to your own GPS?

CHAPTER 22

YOUR JOURNEY

Barbara Grace Reynolds

Being guided by the light is a never-ending process. I am always asking questions of my guidance and getting answers. I have so many note pads and also computer documents where I have recorded the responses that I get. I was looking over some of the channeled messages that I recorded over the years and I can see how I am still getting answers to those same messages. It is like we are always moving up and so we get more and more information as we release the old beliefs and are ready to accept more. Here are some examples of my own questions and answers from years gone by. My Guidances parts are in italics.

12/16/10

What daily practice can I do to make soulness my natural response instead of humanness. How do I make that switch?

Beloved, connecting with us is part of that transition. Spending time in meditation also helps with that transition. Being aware and mindful also helps with that transition. Setting the intention each morning will also help with that transition. You are already doing many things to make this so. Release any known blocks that you may have to being more spiritual and less physical. Yes, you feel that resistance within you now. Release that and notice when others come up.

1/12/11

You are seeing how things work when you are going with the flow that you have created. You are seeing that it is not happening outside of you but within you. You are seeing what power you have and how to use that power for your own greatest good as well as the greatest good of others. You are shifting from looking out there to creating within. This is all good.

Is there something that I should add to what I am doing or anything that I need to clear?

> *You already know the answers. You have the access to all of the answers to all questions. Recognize that connection and allow yourself to accept the knowledge in every moment. You do have the ability to be more, much more. You must allow the flow. It is not just around you but also within you. It is the flow of **All**.*
>
> *Today when you recognized that you were coming from fear and doubt you could have instantly changed that. Why did you not? What are you afraid of? I guess I was afraid it wouldn't work and then I would be feeling good for no reason. As I am typing this I see how silly that is. How can any moment of happiness ever be a waste of time? Lol Exactly! As you allow more and more happiness into your life in each moment, you create more and more happiness to come into your life in each moment. This is the law of attraction.*
>
> *It is much like the conversations you have been having of late. Recognizing and allowing yourself to be the powerful being that you are. No longer coming from what society has taught you. Stepping into your own truth. That is what the energy of this year is about. Some will accept this challenge and some will back away. It does not matter what is decided since everyone will come into their power or leave this earthly plane. That is the choice.*
>
> *So, when we let go of the need to judge we are also opening up even more and allowing ourselves to create without limits? Yes, very much so. It is the knowing that brings you the power. When you come from that knowing, and ignore or release those little fearful thoughts, then you are firmly accepting your power and creating what you desire. You know it is to be so because that is what you have decided.*

I have done my intentions and it feels right, for now. What should I do next?

> *Be clear about what you really want in your life. You are accepting your own power and so what you desire will manifest quicker and easier than ever before. Know what you want.*

1/8/13

> *This is a time of great change. A time when you will become more and more aware of who you really are. A time when you will have so many opportunities to release and let go of the past. A time to realize that the fate of the world does not rest on you but resides within you. A time to see that you are the co-creator of your reality and the one you co-create*

*with is **You**. So all attachments with the real world are an illusion. All problems and issues are an illusion. All physical existence is an illusion. Everything you have been taught to value or see as important is an illusion. This Knowing gives you the freedom to create and experience more. To create and experience all of the beauty and wonder that your heart desires. It gives you the freedom to be all that you have ever wanted to be and more. The freedom to live your dreams. The freedom to change your life. The freedom to step out in power and love. All that you have ever asked for is already yours. Open up and receive the unending supply of Love which you are. **Be Love - Now!***

7/13/13

You have taught me so much! And I really do appreciate it. Now I am apparently learning to truly stand in my own power and creations and allow others to do the same.

3/29/16

I find it interesting that what I mentioned in my last message is what I am still going through two years later. So much in my life and within me has changed. I just wonder what are the major things that I need to release today?

Beloved, you are undergoing a major shift in your life and in your beliefs. You know this. It has been happening for quite some time. We make this as easy for you as possible by guiding you to new and better ways of releasing. You are here to show the world how to change and this means that you have to change first. This builds your trust in your own abilities and your Team (Guides). You have come a long way. Life is a never ending journey, and you know this. Do not ever think that you will never make it to the end. There is no end. Everything is constantly changing and so there is never an ending. This is why we encourage you and all others to focus on the next step instead of the end of the journey. This is also why we say that you cannot get it wrong. There is no wrong, there is only what is.

We know that it is sometimes difficult for you to wrap your mind around all that we share with you. But you also see that with time it all falls into sense. You begin to understand the new thought patterns that are being established. You begin to speak the language.

For today, let go of the need to know everything at once. Let go of the need to hold back until you do understand. As you move forward in your understanding, you will understand more and more. We know that this may not make sense to your logical mind but your heart knows of what we speak. Trust in your heart and release what does not fit with your heart's wisdom. You are doing fine and things are changing for the better. You are taking your focus off of the world and putting it on what you have the control and power over, your own thoughts and life. This is where everyone is moving so keep moving so you can show others the way. This is the ultimate solutions that all others seek. Allow yourself to gain the knowledge and skills to make a bigger and bigger difference in this world. All is well. Release and let go.

I hope reading some of what I have gone through helps you to see that you are doing fine. Everyone is going through the process of learning who they really are and how to live in this new state of Knowing. There is no deadline or punishment for not achieving perfection. Where ever you are on your path is exactly where you are on your path. There is no meaning attached to it, except for the meaning that you are giving it.

Remember that you are on a never ending journey. You will ask questions and get answers. Over time when you go back and read the answers from the past, you may find that they have more or deeper means. This is because you are evolving. This is one of the reasons that Guidance says not to compare yourself to anyone else. We are each on our own unique path and each of those paths is guiding us to the Light.

Chapter 23

Channeled messages from those Who see

Jennifer Del Villar

Blessings to those who allow us to speak gently into your soul and spirit. We come in peace and love. We come to cherish that which you are and to shine light into your beings; not to harm, not to judge, not to belittle but to bring hope, help, insight, and knowing. We say unto you magnificent beings of the earthly plane, be at peace and know that we are one with you. Yes, we are in a different space in this sphere; but we are one. No "one" is ever not connected to another. We are energy; strings of time and particles that create a mesh of webs which align in brilliance. Light upon light, you are sacred.

We are messengers who have come to soothe your weariness, bring you truth, and awaken you from your hypnotic state. We are connected, yet detached, allowing us to see from a higher perspective. We are distanced from that which weighs you down as it does not sit upon our beings. We know each is walking their path to the truth of all; but all paths have both briars and blooms. We **See** you and **Hear** you and **Acknowledge** you in your journey and wish to stand with you and comfort you in the rocky times and in the brilliant splendor.

For some, we feel questioning and pondering of that which has little true meaning in the vastness of the entirety of all. We see you cloaked in sadness in this existence as you question how in the end it may have been for naught. Your brain creates a forest of overgrown and thorny limbs of thoughts and feelings in which you feel entrapped and find yourself tumbling into a place where you see no joy or meaning. Where daily existence focuses on just getting by and where restless evening slumber awakens you into a morning of what you perceive to be as stepping into a coffin. You drink a daily cup of cruelness within the poisoned thoughts of your own mind and beg for respite. We say unto you, come into us, come home, and let us give you peace and hope.

Others we see covering themselves in the cloths of kings but who inwardly see themselves as peasants. While neither the king nor the peasant is greater or lesser than the other (it's simply their journey of the time), you see a difference. You have become a sacred spirit painted in a tomb of adornment seeking adoration while hiding within a veil of self-loathing and defeat. An actor who plays a part in a play to which they act but do embrace the playwright. We say unto you, come into us, come home, and let us introduce you to the part you have always been born to play... yourself.

Oh those who are so concerned with the happiness of another that they treat themselves with maliciousness and disrespect. To their temperate souls, love and honoring self is perceived as selfishness. These are the ones who would allow their own dreams and hopes to fade into a background becoming white noise. But when the pinnacle of utter frustration and bitterness claws its way to the surface, they lash out with a tongue the burns with the intensity of grandest fire-breathing dragon. We say unto you, come into us, come home, and let us show you the path that leads to your own resurrection.

To the one who seeks to be the perfect sculpture and allows others, rather than self, to mold the clay of their existence. They who would refuse to live their underlying truth based upon the dictation of another. They who beat up their spirit in a constant struggle to say the right thing, do the right thing, be the right thing, and ultimately force themselves in a box of limitedness instead of limitlessness. We say unto you, come into us, come home, and let us show you the path that leads to joyful imperfection of true self.

We see those that are terrified of the hidden ghosts that haunt then in a cape of worry, but that truly do not exist. In a shell of fear they dance upon their own beautiful mysteries filled with fright, nervousness, and tepidness. While they do not see it, feel it, or allow it, they truly possess the assuredness and strength of a hurricane within their breast. We say unto you, come into us, come home, and let us show you the soul of the lion that awaits release within your spirit.

Dear souls, who believe they live in a state of madness; who imagine that underneath every thought that they acknowledge lies a creation of illusion and untruth; that the essence of their being is that which comes from an interpretation of insanity, we say unto you, come into us, come home, and allow your visions to create an adventure that is of magic, reality and beauty.

We see the one who "know all" and feel no need to question anything; not out of the gentleness of knowing or teaching, but of needing to sew superiority into their being. Where knowledge is used as a tool to destroy rather than construct; to belittle instead of uplift. Who in their own brilliance create an air of dominance. We say unto you, come into us, come home, and let us show you the meaning of a knowledge that surpasses all understanding.

And then there are the task masters who would take upon themselves to rule others and themselves. To define that which should be and that which should not be. Beings that use control as a blanket to soothe their ravaged and weary spirit. Who use anger and malice to crush their opponent, when their true opponent is their own soul. We say unto you, come into us, come home, lay down your false power and come into the sanctification of your truth.

We know that you hold within your beings one, or multiple, characteristics of that which we have spoken. These are patterns of the past and the now which were given for your growth. Each and every soul who has and will exist has shattered pieces within themselves that in self-love and recognition need to skillfully be placed back into the glorious pattern of self which will allow the masterpiece to be re-exhibited.

Oh my beauties - do you not know that which you are? You are magical, brilliant, light-filled vibrational creations? You are time travelers who bring about change, who forge vibrational shifts and carry forth the destiny of hope. You are the dreamers, the inventors, the creatives, the torchbearers, the nurturers! You are all children and all ancients; you have existed from the beginning and will continue to exist. While the energy shifts, you still are.

Hold yourself in esteem, separate from ego, and know your purpose is that of majesty. You are the chosen one; we are the chosen ones. The ones who ride the waves of the sea on the back of a magical sea creature and dive deep into the waters of time and space. Your destiny is of unending love that crosses all time, space and lands. Lands where anything can be imagined. Lands where a purple dragon can fly and a fairy can dine on candied figs with platypuses.

To live triumphantly is a choice you make daily; the contract entered at the beginning of all that was remains eternally. Our greatest hope is that you shall wake up and exalt that which you've come into. A "world" where there are no boundaries. A world in which you are a flower that blooms and when nourishment is needed the skies open up to lovingly feed your soul with waters of universal manna. You will receive that which you require when it is required.

To bring you to that truth, we bear witness to the importance of time to nurture you. That in the quiet of the time when nature's painter covers the atmosphere in greys and darkness; be silent and go within. In the time when morning's sun peaks beyond the veil to guide the lightness forth; be silent and go within. In the weaning and waning hours in the middle of the time keeper's daily walk through the hours, take moments for your needs. Dignify your soul with moments of retrospection to remember the meaning of who you are. If you can find yourself within, you will better understand that which you are – what we all are – because we are one. And ask of us to join in your presence so that if you do delve into the lies that you hold of yourself, we can gently and lovingly sweep away those thoughts with the broom of source's grace.

As we leave you please remember beloved, the stars are your children and the moon is your mother. The blade of grass that dances in the breeze calls you sister or brother, and the sparrow that glides is one with your being. In this gift of existence we would ask that you open your heart to all that you truly are. Let that which doesn't serve and hinders you, fall away gratefully and graciously like the chaff from the wheat. Believe that universe is ushering in experiences, dreams and vibrations that allow your soul to flourish in a land of creativity, invention, imagination, joy, playfulness, intuition, trust, connection, empathy, love, peace, hope, light and self-respect.

Know thyself and love thyself; for in knowing and loving thyself you know and love us and all. You are home in us anytime you choose; call upon us and we will not be distant. We love you.

Conclusion

There has always existed communication between the earth plane and other spiritual realms. Many believed that only those few who were gifted psychically could receive telepathic communications through the veil between these dimensions. These gifted people were often regarded as either religious prophets or insane deviants. At any rate, they were certainly not viewed as normal. Sort of like myself! Nowadays, this is a topic where people's attitudes and understanding are changing and shifting.

With a new spiritual awakening and a new energy flooding the planet, telepathic communication with Angelic and Spirit Guides and other celestial beings is becoming more and more common. When we seek guidance with sincerity in our hearts, messages come to us in many forms and in many ways. There is a new opening of the human consciousness at this point in time, and we have the opportunity to expand the way in which we see, hear, and feel by seeking inner guidance with our higher self and our Guides. We have the ability to make connections through the veil that have not been possible on such a large scale until now. The potential of these divine connections are life-changing.

The increase in the vibrations on the planet is having a profound effect on people. Those who are particularly sensitive are feeling the need for adjustment and change. Those who are psychically active are receiving guidance and specific instructions on how to prepare themselves and how to help guide others. The planet is changing quickly, partly due to the activities of humans and partly due to the new ray of energy bringing in this higher vibration. The key for us in this time of great transition is to turn within for guidance; humanity as a whole has the opportunity to realize this and benefit from Angelic communication. We all have the ability to turn inward for assistance and meditation and prayer are essential tools in this spiritual awakening process.

If we are open and mindful of our spirituality while we are proceeding with work on the physical plane we will find diverse ways of applying our spiritual practices. Conversely, by operating with integrity and selflessness on the material level, we bring strength and integrity to our spiritual work. We can turn inward to seek guidance with problems and challenges we face in the outer world. We can find Angelic signs and guideposts in our surroundings that will guide us in our inner pursuits for serenity and happiness. The two are one: our inner work and our outer work flow together. Our journey upon the awakened path is one which includes progress in our spiritual pursuits and progress in our everyday activities. By reaching out to your Spirit Guides and Angels, you strengthen the bond and open the door to so many possibilities. They are here to assist in your awakening and spiritual development on every step of the journey.

Take each day and regard it as a jewel unto itself. We must admire all its facets, all its variations, and consider each moment here on earth as precious. By doing the very best we can, no matter what our priorities no matter what our responsibilities, open the possibility of greater love and gratitude in our lives. The jewel holds within it both the material and the spiritual aspects. We must first however, effect these changes within ourselves and become comfortable with functioning from our heart area in all we do. Love and compassion must fill our lives and surround every activity we undertake. This is the natural progression of the energy on earth right now. If we align our personal wills with unconditional love and acceptance, we can make in-depth and successful changes in our lives.

As we continue slowly, steadily on the illumined path, we find that we are eliminating from our lives all that is associated with low vibrations. Such acts as lying, manipulating, cheating, stealing, and willfully injuring others we can no longer do without instant regret. As we change more of our cells to accept the higher vibrational rate, we completely clear the possibility of such actions from our natures, from our very beings. Instead, our actions and reactions include compassion, forgiveness, selfless service, understanding, and unconditional love. These then become part of our makeup as we move further, step by step, on our illumined and awakened path.

Once we begin on this path, it is crucial to regard these communications with our Spiritual Team as sacred and prepare ourselves for the fact that we may need to continue this process for years before we attain an enlightened state with our entire being. Until that time comes, you will be rewarded with clarity and wisdom beyond your current knowledge as well as compassion and love for all.

Make it a habit to communicate with your Angelic Guides on a regular basis. Develop the relationship as you would with a new friendship. Strengthen the bonds between you and watch how your life changes in a positive and uplifting manner.

I promise, once you start your journey to connect with spirit, beautiful synchronicities will appear again and again.

Sending much love and light to all. xx

Jewels

Co-Authors Bio's and Photos

Jewels Rafter is a Best-Selling Author, International Clairvoyant, Medium, Spiritual Life Coach, Healer, and Radio Host who has been living her passion for over fifteen years. She specializes in Clairvoyant & Intuitive Readings, Mediumship, Angelic Readings, Reiki, Crystal Healing, Life Coaching, and Spiritual Counseling. Being the owner and CEO of Harmony Radio, as well as her own company – Ohm Readings & Therapies, Jewels presents others with the opportunity to connect with Spirit and find guidance and clarity along their life journey. She provides people with the necessary tools to grow spiritually, and move forward along the path of inner enlightenment. She truly believes that when you live in your own light, everything flows.

www.ohmreadings.ca
www.facebook.com/OhmReadings
ohmreadings@outlook.com

Brian D. Calhoun is a Heart-Centered International Psychic-Medium who has dedicated his life to bringing messages of love & light for the purposes of healing & enlightenment to people around the world for over fifteen years. Also a Reiki Master-Teacher, Ordained Minister, Chef and Certified Personal Fitness Trainer, Brian will often use is intuitive gifts and abilities to guide people to live a light, healthy and trim life in all ways. Born and raised literally in the City with the Heart of Gold, Timmins, Ontario, Brian has called Ottawa, Ontario home since 1995. He has released a Meditation CD, has written multiple published articles, appeared on local television and has been featured on International Radio.

www.angelswithin.ca
www.facebook.com/angelswithin

Tracie Mahan is a Psychic Medium, Clairvoyant, Hypnotherapist, Family Coach, NLP Practitioner, QHHT Practitioner, and Reiki Master. For the past two decades, she has dedicated herself to her personal path of spiritual and psychic development. Tracie comes from a highly sensitive and intuitive family and has fortified her natural gifts with training and practice, enabling her to connect with guides, angels, Ascended Masters, and spiritual council. In addition to being a clear channel of messages from these realms, her expertise also includes offering clients a perspective through looking at past lives to identify important connections with the present incarnation.

www.traciemahan.com
www.facebook.com/traciemahancht

Kimla Dodds is a Radio Host and is currently working on her doctorate degree in Metaphysical Counseling from the University of Sedona. She is certified in Astrology (Western and Chinese) Mediumship, Tarot, Light Resonance Healing and is a Feng Shui Practitioner. Psychic since childhood, she has worked to accelerate balanced living through counseling services while sharing her knowledge. Kimla's passion and crusade is highlighting the awareness of unseen energy. She is an ongoing contributor to the non-profit charity foundation of "Recording for the Blind." Kimla currently resides in Phoenix, Arizona and enjoys traveling the globe teaching, learning, and experiencing this wonderful and challenging world called life.

www.kimladodds.com
kimla@kimladodds.com

Wendy James has been a professional international psychic and holistic practitioner since 1994. She is trained in numerous oracle and divination techniques with an extensive knowledge of metaphysical studies from diversified and qualified instructors. Her specialties include Reiki Master, IET Therapist, Crystal Practitioner, International Master Psychic, Ordained Pagan High Priestess & Spiritual Advisor.

www.luvdragons.ca

Being an overachiever from a young age, Josée Leduc is a Certified Spiritual Coach, and Meditation Instructor, Reiki Master as well as a dedicated mother and wife. On her spiritual journey, she is dedicated to helping others achieve their potential through a more personal approach. Her passion and enthusiasm truly empowers her students by providing them with the tools they required to evolve spiritually. She believes that every human being can enhance their experience on earth by reconnecting with their inner light. Josée Leduc is definitely a positive force that helps people embrace life and live to the fullest.

puresoul@live.ca

Roni Campbell is seventy years old, married, and lives in Kelowna, BC. She was born in Hamilton, Ontario, and lived in London, Montreal, and Whitehorse as her father was in the Canadian Armed Forces. Her first marriage was at nineteen years old and from this union was born a son. Roni spent forty-three years with her husband Johnnie, who has passed away in 2014. Roni and her husband fostered forty-five children and also had a thriving seasonal fudge business that took them to many Home Shows. She has a background in administration and real estate. In June 2014, Roni was remarried to a lovely man named Tom whom she is currently enjoying retirement with. Roni's passion is photography, nature, camping and fishing.

www.facebook.com/profile.php?id=100008334221631&fref=ts
roni.campbell2014@gmail.com

Anu Shi Asta is an internationally known spiritual teacher, Atlantean intuitive, Author (*Journey to the World of Angels* and *Creating Heaven on Earth*, both published in Finland), Radio show host of Heaven on Earth, Creator of Angel Light Hypnosis™, Reiki Master, Past Life Regressionist and a Certified Clinical Hypnotherapist. Angels started coming to her dreams after her first son was born in 1995, revealing her life purpose as a messenger of Light. Ever since the first Angelic contact, she has been on a magical journey that has led her to fearlessly move from Finland to the United States with her two sons while creating a successful spiritual business. She is deeply committed to helping others awaken to their own innate gifts and ancient inner wisdom, and inspiring others to create the life of their dreams.

www.anushiasta.com
www.anushiasta.com/heavenonearth/

Barbara Grace Reynolds is a world renowned Freedom and Empowerment Coach, Infinity Healer, Conscious Channel and Blog Talk Radio Host. She uses her connection with Source to assist others in seeing the greatness within themselves and to release the need to live small. She connects with people individually, in groups, by radio, in books and in many other ways. She loves to see people open up to their own love and the love of God. Her life is filled with Love, Joy and Abundance. She helps thousands of people all over the world.

www.divinelyguidedhealing.com
www.infinityhealingforwomen.com

Tracy Lacroix is a Reiki/ Integrated Energy Therapy Practitioner and Angel card reader. She uses her intuition and angels to guide people on their own healing journey. She is dedicated to helping others by volunteering as a Peer Support Worker for domestic violence and a strong activist for Violence against Women. She assists seniors who have cognitive disabilities (Dementia and Alzheimer's) at an Adult Day Program, and helps out the homeless. When Tracy is not serving others, she enjoys being out in nature, reading and meditating. She is a true survivor! She knows anything is possible if you believe in yourself!

www.facebook.com/profile.php?id=100011188629894
butterfly-blessings@hotmail.com

Gabriella Studor's journey started in May 2010 when she had her Spiritual Awakening after giving birth to her second child. During a walk with her husband and beautiful new baby, they noticed a sign for Angel Card Readings. Her husband suggested she get a Reading! Gabriella was told she was a "Healer and Messenger". She was guided to learn a hands on healing modality called Reiki. Gabriella connected with her Angels and is presently an Angel Intuitive and channel for Angelic Healing. Her healing modalities include Integrated Energy Therapy, Karuna Reiki, and Access Bars.

www.healingfromabove.ca
www.facebook.com/healingfromabovegabriella

Jennifer (Jen) Del Villar is a writer, singer/songwriter and eternal optimist out of Portland, Oregon. Jen has an empathic connection with all individuals, but is drawn to the musical and artistic tribes. In her mid-twenties, Jen had the experience of receiving the gift of speaking in tongues opened in her through the laying upon of hands. Jen has experience being a channel (though not the only one) for the Goddess Freja who can communicate through this gift. In the journey of the gift of life, Jen's mission is to illuminate the incredible, mystical, beautiful, worthy soul that each individual possesses on this path and all paths to come.

www.Jenniferdelvillar.com
Jenelisedv@gmail.com

Michele O'Reggio is a courageous Cancerian and a gentle warrior who practices radical self-care. She is a catalyst for change, inspiring and empowering others to let go of what no longer serves them and to see the possibilities ahead. Life lessons and deep self-discovery helped Michele discover her unique soul gifts. She is a Certified Angel Card Reader™ and an intuitive channel for Divine guidance and healing. Michele empowers others to tune into their Divine radiance so they can discover their life purpose and live with more joy, love and inner peace.

https://www.facebook.com/groups/iamradiant
iamradiantandloved@gmail.com

Deb Bergersen is a mom, grandmother, great-grandmother, a wife to a loving husband, a sister, an aunt and great-aunt. She spent years of her life in pursuit of an outside source of spirituality, only to find that spirituality was inside of her. That search opened her eyes to all the wonderful possibilities in life. Her free time is spent exploring, photographing nature and ancient ruins. She is also uses Reiki mostly for family and friends. Her goal in life is to live it fully.

https://www.facebook.com/DebsTimePassages/
madjest211@yahoo.com

Maureen Sullivan has had an innate understanding of the healing power of energy since very young and has been practicing energy work for the past eight years. She is a registered Reflexologist, Reiki Master/Teacher and an Integrated Energy Therapy Practitioner. Her experience as a women and children's counselor has given her a unique combination of understanding the heart and body's energy field. Maureen feels a strong spiritual connection to the earth and believes in the healing power of the Great Mother in helping us to balance and connect to ourselves!

www.treeoflifehealing.ca
maureen.morningdove@gmail.com

Julie Dudley is a mom of two who grew up in Lac Brome, Québec. She's always had a deep love for the outdoors, angels, fairies, nature, and animals. She's very passionate about healing, crystals, card readings, and rune stones. She offers Reiki sessions and gives card readings in her home in Gatineau, Québec.

www.mystiquedreams.com

Christine Gilmour is a Reiki Master & IET Master Instructor offering sessions/classes in Ottawa. She loves teaching others how to tune into their own inner wisdom and intuition. Certified Angel Intuitive Practitioner by Doreen Virtue, she offers angelic healing bringing through positive messages of love and support from the Angels.

https://www.hearlight-therapies.com

Vanessa Krichbaum is a heart centered, holistic, financial advisor. She finds enormous satisfaction in helping her clients align their finances with their values and dreams. At all times, she is meticulous with each step in the planning process, to ensure the highest good for the client, family, business and the world.

www.facebook.com/profile.php?id=561027020&fref=ts

Helen Cline is a Psychic intuitive, Tarot and Oracle card reader. She is a radio show host as well as a psychic adviser on "Living in the Light" page on Facebook. Helen is a straight shooter with her readings and is changing the world in wonderful ways with her work.

www.HelensIntuitiveInsights.com

Erica Johansen currently resides in Oregon with her children. She has worked in the healing-arts field for over ten years as a Massage therapist and now a Reiki practitioner. In her free time when she's not chasing kids, she enjoys hiking, ecstatic dancing and is passionate about helping others.

massage.byerica@yahoo.com

Compiled by Jewels Rafter

CPSIA information can be obtained
at www.ICGtesting.com
Printed in the USA
LVOW12s0351310716
498142LV00001B/4/P